Jewelry Making for Beginners:
32 Projects with Metals

GRETA PACK

Dover Publications, Inc.
Mineola, New York

Bibliographical Note

This Dover edition, first published in 2007, is a slightly altered republication of the work published by D. Van Nostrand Co., Princeton, 1957, under the title *Jewelry Making for the Beginning Craftsman*. The Dover edition omits the section "Sources of Supply" from the Van Nostrand edition. The endpapers of the Dover edition have been reproduced from those in the Van Nostrand edition.

Library of Congress Cataloging-in-Publication Data

Pack, Greta.
    Jewelry making for beginners: 32 projects with metals / Greta Pack.
       p. cm.
    "First published in 2007, is a slightly altered republication of the work published by D. Van Nostrand Co., Princeton, 1957, under the title Jewelry Making for the Beginning Craftsman."
    ISBN-13: 978-0-486-46041-3
    ISBN-10: 0-486-46041-X
    1. Jewelry making—Amateurs' manuals. 2. Metal-work—Amateurs; manuals. I. Pack, Greta. Jewelry making for the beginning craftsman. II. Title.

TT212.P32 2007
745.594'2—dc22

                                     2007013843

Manufactured in the United States of America
Dover Publications, Inc., 31 East 2nd Street, Mineola, N.Y. 11501

To
LOUISE L. GREEN

JEWELRY MAKING FOR BEGINNERS

is a work manual for children who wish to make jewelry of silver and other metals. It will introduce them to the skills and processes of an ancient and honorable craft which has unlimited possibilities.

An interesting feature of this type of craft work is that from the beginning, with a few essential tools, materials, and simple working drawings, one can learn to make really wearable jewelry. As in any craft, practice is necessary in order to acquire the workmanship which will give good results. To this end the processes used are repeated many times.

The projects in this book are not given in order of difficulty, but those which combine similar decorative processes have been grouped together.

For best use of space, directions for the processes have not been repeated, but reference pages may be found with each project.

It will be noted that a number of the articles are made of units which can be combined in various ways to make new designs. The transition from these projects to independent planning can be accomplished by experimenting with units of metal which vary in size, shape and texture until a good workable design has been arranged. Then the sequence of the processes will be determined and the working plan made. In this way, the beginner will build up a knowledge of the craft which will inspire him to do more finished work.

Contents

Metals

Several inexpensive metals, both in sheet and wire form, can be used to make interesting jewelry. For the beginner, copper and brass are recommended because of their low cost, but even advanced jewelers who work almost exclusively in sterling silver frequently use copper and brass for variety and color.

As far as construction is concerned, all the metals named can be used interchangeably for the jewelry included in this book. When the beginning craftsman becomes more skillful he may want to work more often in sterling silver which, although it costs a little more, is a fine adaptable metal.

The different metals vary in hardness. Annealing is a heating process which is given to the metal to make it soft and pliable. Most of the metals used for the following projects may be purchased annealed. If the metal has to be annealed, lay it on a screen and hot plate until the heat turns it a glowing red, then set it aside to cool or plunge it into water for quick cooling. *Use only annealed sheet and wire for the following projects.*

COPPER is used in its pure metallic state. Its reddish-brown color gives it a warm outdoor quality. Cold rolled and annealed sheet is smooth and easy to work. It can be polished and lacquered for a permanent finish.

BRASS is an alloy of copper and zinc, harder than copper. It is gold in color. It takes a high polish and is lacquered to preserve the luster.

STERLING SILVER is an alloy of pure silver and a small percentage of another metal, usually copper, to harden it. It is a more precious metal than copper or brass, it is easy to work and can be finished in several different ways; polished for a soft luster, given a high polish, oxidized for depth of color and then polished for highlights.

IRON is taken from iron ore and, when treated, is both tough and flexible and can be pulled into wire. The black iron binding wire referred to in this book is used not only to hold pieces together for soldering, but also for a chain of iron units held together with silver links. If lacquered, the iron will not rust and its dark color and dull texture contrast well with the other metals used.

TIN has the whiteness of silver and is used in many important alloys, among them being solder. We employ tin only for solder, in pure state or alloyed with lead.

1

Bench equipment

Bench vise, used to hold various tools during working operations.

Steel anvil block, a hammering surface on which to smooth or flatten metal.

Lead block, used for many cutting and doming processes.

Clamps, to hold the bench pin in place.

Metal gauge, for measuring the thickness of wire and flat metal.

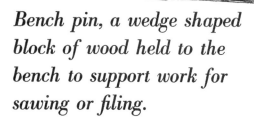

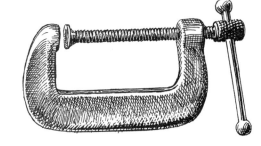

Bench pin, a wedge shaped block of wood held to the bench to support work for sawing or filing.

Tools

Essential tools for the beginner include those here and those on the following four pages. A variety of articles can be made with a small set of good tools; in fact, some of the pieces are made with only two or three of the tools listed. All tools should be kept clean and protected from pressure that may bend or dull them and from moisture which will cause corrosion or rust. A good workman takes care of his tools.

CARE OF TOOLS

Keep the working surface of the steel hammer and steel surface plate free of scratches and dents by using coarse and fine abrasives depending upon the depth of the dent or scratch.

The steel burnisher must be kept well polished and wrapped in chamois skin when not in use.

The file and handle come separately. Only the small files, such as the needle files, have a handle as part of the file. The teeth of the files will become dull if allowed to rub against each other, or against other steel tools. Clean the files with a file brush, and rub the smaller files with a coarse cloth. Files should be put away clean.

Gauges are tools to measure the thickness of the metal sheet and the diameter of the wire. Insert the metal sheet or wire in the slot nearest to the thickness of the metal or diameter of the wire and read the gauge number. The gauge numbers referred to in this book are measured by the Brown and Sharpe Gauge.

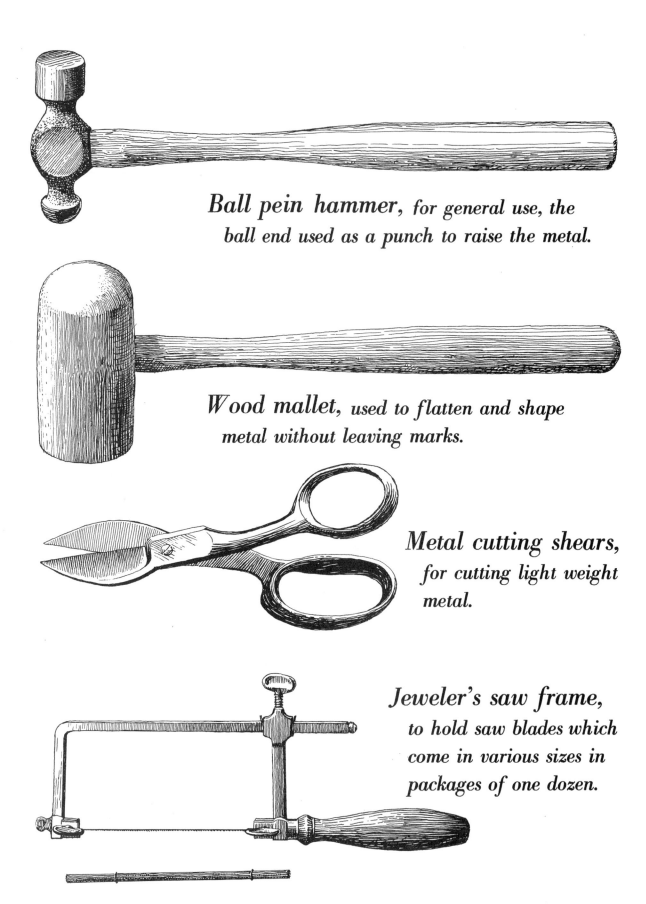

Ball pein hammer, *for general use, the ball end used as a punch to raise the metal.*

Wood mallet, *used to flatten and shape metal without leaving marks.*

Metal cutting shears, *for cutting light weight metal.*

Jeweler's saw frame, *to hold saw blades which come in various sizes in packages of one dozen.*

Hand drill, *to hold and turn the twist drills for drilling holes in metal.*

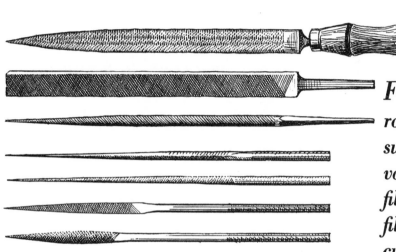

Files, *used to remove rough edges or irregular surfaces. Most useful are various types of needle files and four to six inch files, second or smooth cut.*

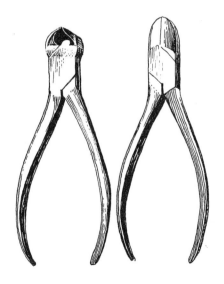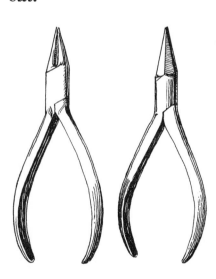

Hand vise, *to hold small work while filing, etc.*

End and side cutting nippers, *used to cut wire.*

Round and square nose pliers, *used to bend and form wire.*

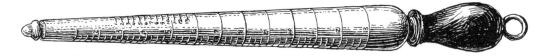

Ring making tools

Ring mandrel, a slightly tapered spindle used in forming rings.
Ring gauge, used in measuring ring sizes.
Ring sizes, a series of graduated rings marked with standard sizes to measure the fingers.
Ring clamp, to hold rings firmly for filing or stone setting.

Disk cutting and doming tools

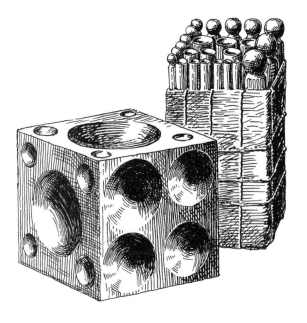

Dapping die, a metal block with depressions into which metal can be dapped into rounded forms.

Dapping die cutters, tools with cutting ends, used to cut disks.
Dapping die punches, domed steel tools used to raise metal disks in the dapping die.

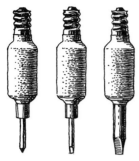

Soldering tools

Electric soldering iron, used to heat the metal and melt soft solder.

Soldering tweezers, to clamp pieces together for soldering. Cotter pins, to hold small parts together for soldering. Iron binding wire, to bind parts firmly while soldering.

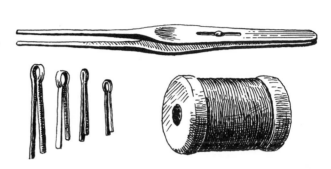

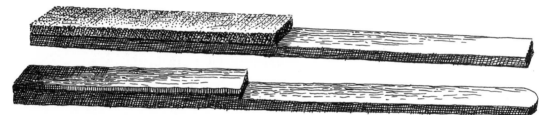

Finishing and polishing tools

Hand buffs, felt and chamois on wood handles, to buff and polish metal. Steel burnisher, used to smooth and finish metal.

Tweezers, used to handle stones and small objects. Scriber, used to mark an inscribed line on metal. Center punch, used to make depressions in the metal. Dividers, used to inscribe circles and divide lines.

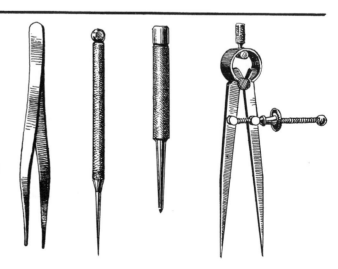

7

The Basic Processes

Following are the basic processes for all jewelry making. Cleaning and filing keep the metal in condition for sawing and soldering which are construction processes, and for wire working which is a decorative process. Polishing and lacquering are finishing processes which bring out the technique of construction, and if well done, enhance the beauty of the article.

Sawing

Sawing with a jeweler's saw blade set in a jeweler's saw frame is used for metals which are too heavy in gauge or too intricate in pattern to be cut with shears. This type of saw can be used for straight, curved or angular lines which often form the outline and shape of the design. The saw blade comes in several different sizes. The coarsest used in this book is #1 and the finest #0.

The thickness of the metal must be greater than the distance between the teeth of the blade to prevent the metal from becoming wedged between the teeth, and the saws from bending and breaking. For example, saw 18 gauge metal with a #1 saw blade.

Transferring the pattern to the metal

Transfer the traced pattern with carbon paper and a hard pencil.

Scratch the traced design into the metal.

Wipe the metal with a damp cloth to remove the carbon lines.

Setting the blade in the frame

The worker should be directly in front of the V in the bench pin with the shoulder about 3 inches above the bench top.

With the frame in a horizontal position, place the upper arm of the frame in the V of the bench pin. Hold and press the handle against the body and clamp one end of the blade in the lower jaw. Press the frame, clamp the loose end in the upper jaw. Release the pressure. The blade must be taut.

Sawing the pattern

The right arm holding the saw frame vertically should be directly in front of the bench pin.

Use the full length of the blade when sawing straight or curved lines. For angles use the center of the blade with short strokes in one place to make a space in which to turn the blade.

the bench pin
clamped firmly to the bench

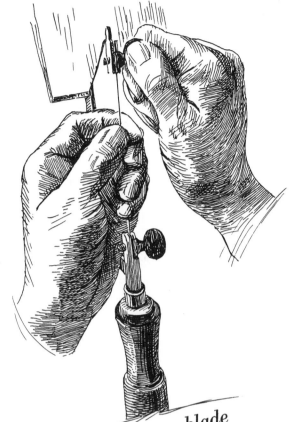

setting the saw blade

Place the blade in the lower jaw, teeth pointing down toward the handle and away from the frame.
Press the arms of the frame toward each other while inserting the blade in the upper jaw.

Saw with a vertical stroke, the blade always perpendicular to the metal.

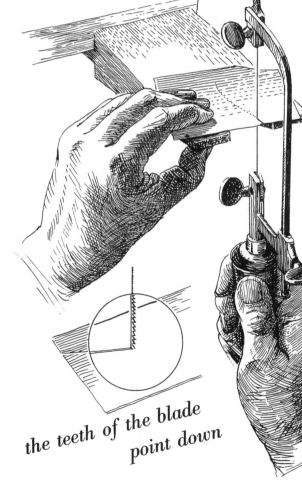

the teeth of the blade
point down

Piercing

Piercing is the term used when the metal is sawed out leaving an openwork design, or when the background is sawed out leaving the design in the metal.

Transfer the pattern to the metal.

Make depressions with the center punch in the sections which are to be pierced.

Insert the twist drill in the chuck of the hand drill and drill holes marked by the punch. Care must be taken in selecting the drill so the size of the hole will not destroy the traced line of the design.

Set the saw blade in the lower jaw of the saw frame.

Thread the blade through the drilled hole nearest the center of the design.

Support the metal against the lower jaw of the frame while inserting the loose end of the blade in the upper jaw of the frame.

Saw out the section. Follow the directions under sawing.

Return the saw frame to the horizontal position.

Loosen the blade from the upper jaw, and remove from the pierced section.

Insert the end as before through another drilled hole.

Repeat as above until the design or the background has been pierced.

Transferring the pattern, p. 8. *Sawing*, p. 8.

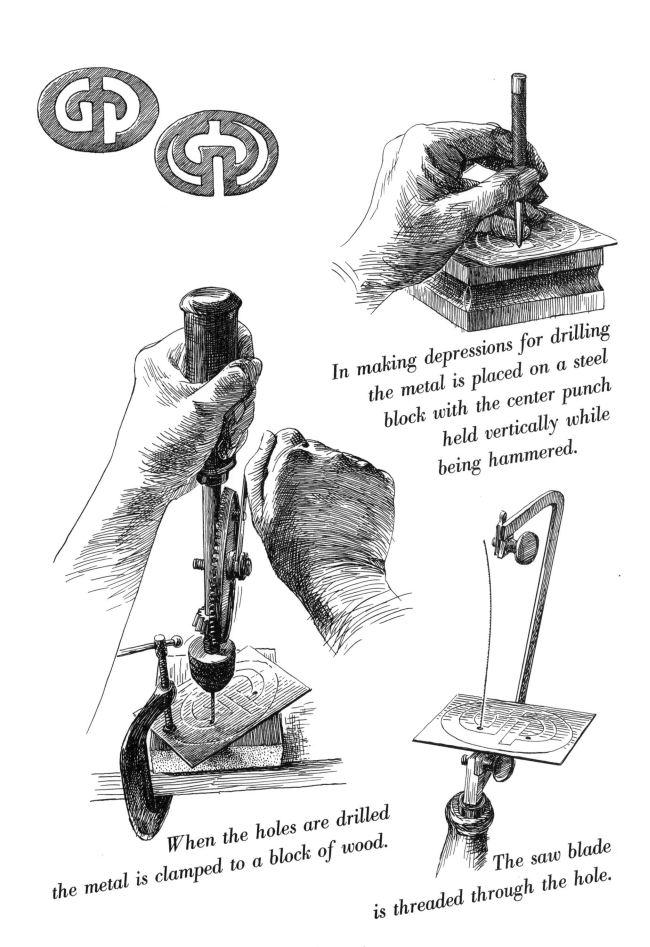

In making depressions for drilling the metal is placed on a steel block with the center punch held vertically while being hammered.

When the holes are drilled the metal is clamped to a block of wood.

The saw blade is threaded through the hole.

Filing

Filing is used to smooth rough edges, to level irregular surfaces and remove excess solder. The files most commonly used for jewelry work are needle files which come in a variety of shapes designed for various contours and angles. Large files from four to six inches in length come with a tang to be fitted into a wooden handle. These files are used for larger areas or when a greater amount of metal has to be filed away. They can also be used for finishing an edge as they come in both coarse and smooth cut. It is good to have an assortment. Only a few are shown on the tool pages.

Clean the metal with pumice powder.
Place the metal on a steel surface plate.
Tap with a mallet to straighten.
Rub the file lightly with chalk; this helps to keep the teeth
    from becoming filled with metal filings.
Hold the metal firmly.
Put the pressure on the forward stroke, remove the pressure
    on the back stroke to keep the cutting edge of the teeth
    from becoming dull.
Clean the file at intervals.
Remove the burr on the filed edge with a scraper or coarse
    emery cloth.

Cleaning the file, p. 3.

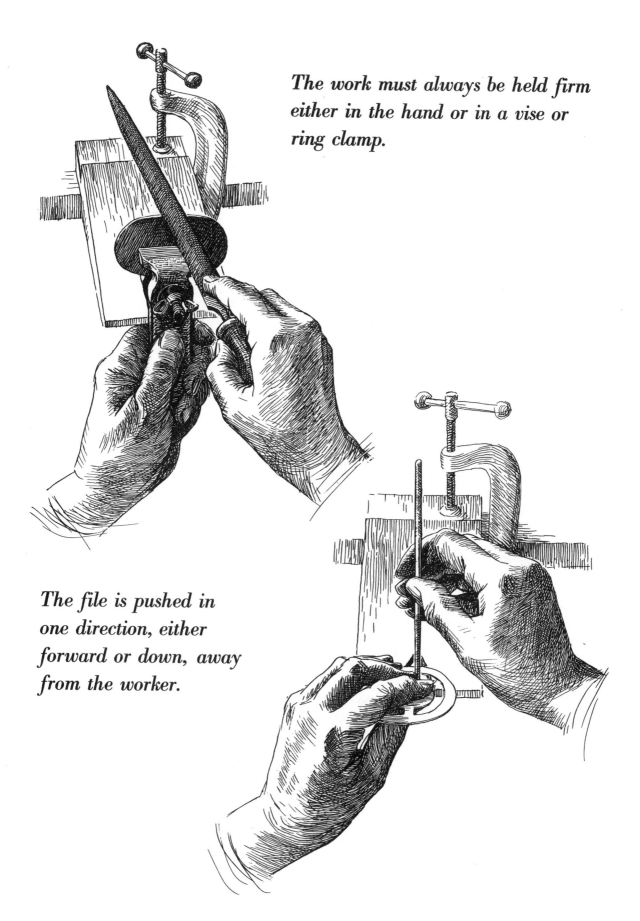

The work must always be held firm either in the hand or in a vise or ring clamp.

The file is pushed in one direction, either forward or down, away from the worker.

13

Soldering

Soldering is a process used to hold metal pieces together by using another metal or combination of metals which melt and flow at a lower temperature than the metal to be joined.

For the following projects soft solder of tin and lead is used. Pure tin is used as solder only with sterling silver, as it is the color of silver and retains its brilliance. To help the flow of the solder and to keep the metal in condition when heated, a substance called flux is necessary. The flux referred to in this book is in paste form.

An electric soldering iron, or electric plate, will heat the metal enough so the solder will flow on the parts to be joined. Wire or small pieces of metal may be soldered with the iron. The electric plate is used for large areas of metal, or that of heavy gauge which cannot be heated enough with the iron. The metal to be joined must be held firmly until it cools.

Soldering irons can be obtained in several different types with replacement tips. The copper tip of the iron must have a thin coating of solder before it can be used. This process is called tinning.

Tinning the iron

Heat the iron. Turn off the electric current.

File the hot tip until it is a bright copper on all surfaces.

Reheat the iron. Rub the hot tip in the flux and solder until a thin coat of solder covers all surfaces of the tip.

Soldering wire joints and small pieces of metal

Hold the metal pieces firmly together.

Pick up the solder with the tip of the iron and place on the joint. Heat the metal until the solder flows.

Sweating a sawed design of metal to a metal background

Clean and flux one side of the metal sheet from which the design is to be sawed. Lay pieces of solder on the fluxed surface. Place on a screen and hot plate until the solder flows. Spread the solder with a hot iron to form a thin coat on the metal. Rinse in water and dry. Saw the design and file all edges smooth.

Clean and flux the background sheet. Clamp the design to the sheet and soldered surface down. Place on a screen and hot plate until the solder melts. This is shown when a thin light line appears between the two metals. Let cool before removing the clamps.

Filing, p. 12. *Transferring the design,* p. 8. *Sawing,* p. 8.

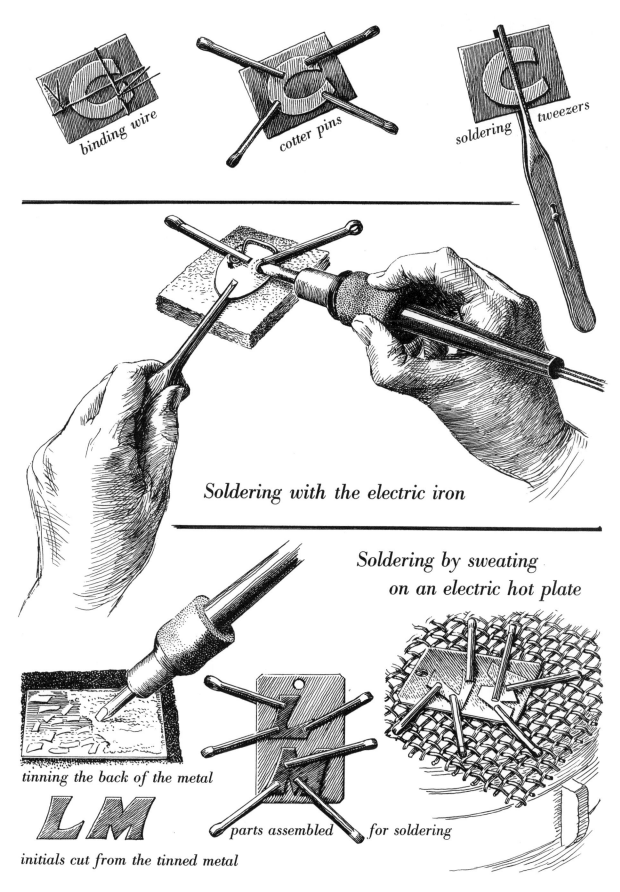

binding wire

cotter pins

soldering tweezers

Soldering with the electric iron

Soldering by sweating
on an electric hot plate

tinning the back of the metal

LM

initials cut from the tinned metal

parts assembled   for soldering

15

Cleaning, Polishing and Finishing

The processes of cleaning, polishing and finishing, as presented in this book, are done by hand without the use of acids or motor driven polishing buffs.

The condition of the metal to be cleaned determines which tool or abrasive should be used first to remove scratches or other defects. Start with the coarsest tool or abrasive necessary and use in succession others finer than the one just used. When smooth and clean, the metal is ready for polishing. The final steps in finishing a piece of jewelry are very important, for if they are done well they will add much to the beauty of the article.

Use tools and abrasives in the following sequence

Clean the metal with fine pumice powder and water, using a soft cloth for flat surfaces and a brush for recessed parts. This will remove discoloration and will show which of the tools or abrasives should be used first.

File in the direction of a deep scratch, using a long stroke with a coarse file, and continue with finer files.

Remove excess solder with a file, scraper or emery cloth.

Remove marks of the file and minor scratches with emery cloth, or scotch stone dipped in water, rubbing in a circular motion to avoid wearing a groove in the metal.

Rub the metal with fine pumice powder and water.

Rub a piece of felt, charged with tripoli cake, over the metal surface (the felt may be mounted on wood and used as a hand buff).

Wash in hot soap suds to remove the oil.

Polishing and finishing

Polish with prepared metal polish for luster.

Rub the curved side of the burnisher over the metal until a high polish has been obtained.

Finish copper and brass with a thin coat of lacquer.

To oxidize sterling silver

Dip the polished silver in a solution of liver of sulphur (a lump about ½ inch in diameter dissolved in a quart of warm water). When the silver becomes dark rinse in cold water. Dry the metal and rub with a soft cloth dipped in whiting or fine pumice powder. Do not lacquer.

Filing, p. 12.

Wire Work

Wire may form the foundation of a piece of jewelry, or it may be applied as a decoration. It is often twisted to add lightness to a design, and can easily be formed into coils or line units of decoration for flat or curved surfaces. Twists and coils of wire can be made of round, half round, or square wire.

Keep the 14 gauge or heavier wire in coils. Wire of a lighter gauge may be wound on spools. If kinks occur in the lighter gauge wire they can be removed by holding the wire ends firmly and the length taut while drawing it over the edge of a wooden bench, or block of wood.

THE JIG

Many of the wire units, coils, and twists shown in this book were made on jigs. The word "jig" is a mechanics' term given to a device which is used to guide a tool or a material. A jig makes the forming of an article easier during construction and makes the finished pieces mechanically more perfect. When a design requires duplication of parts, a jig is often used. The one shown here was made on a block of wood with nails spaced and hammered into the wood, the nail heads sawed off, and the ends made smooth so the wire units may be formed and removed easily.

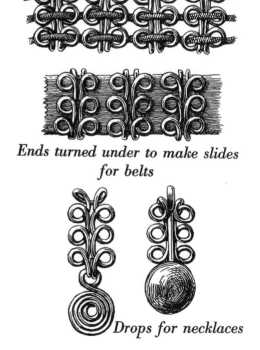

Ends turned under to make slides for belts

Drops for necklaces

Wire unit made on a jig and some of the ways it can be used

17

Wire twisting

Often a design calls for a twist of given length, sometimes a tight or loose twist. To determine the length to cut the wire is important. The gauge of the wire as well as the number of twists the wire is given will determine the length of the finished piece. When round wire is used, two or more lengths are necessary for the twist. A rope-like effect may be obtained by twisting a single length of flat or square wire. *All wire should be annealed.*

Twisting wire 18 gauge or lighter

Measure the amount needed for the twist.

Loop the wire length in the center, and insert the two loose ends through the hole in the spool. Hold the ends in the jaws of a table vise.

Insert a small steel rod through the loop of wire, and pull the wire taut. Hold the spool firmly against the rod. Turn the rod to twist the wire.

Twisting wire 16 gauge or heavier

Hold the looped end of the wire in the jaws of the hand vise. Clamp the loose end in the jaws of the table vise. Turn the hand vise to twist the wire.

To determine the length

In cutting the wire for a definite length of finished twist, the following examples have been given of two round wires of different gauges and lengths.

18 gauge, 26 inches, twisted 50 times, gives 11⅛ inches
18 gauge, 26 inches, twisted 75 times, gives 9⅝ inches
18 gauge, 14 inches, twisted 50 times, gives 5¼ inches
20 gauge, 14 inches, twisted 50 times, gives 4⅞ inches

twisted 14 gauge wire

loosely twisted 18 gauge wire

tightly twisted 18 gauge wire

tightly twisted 20 gauge wire

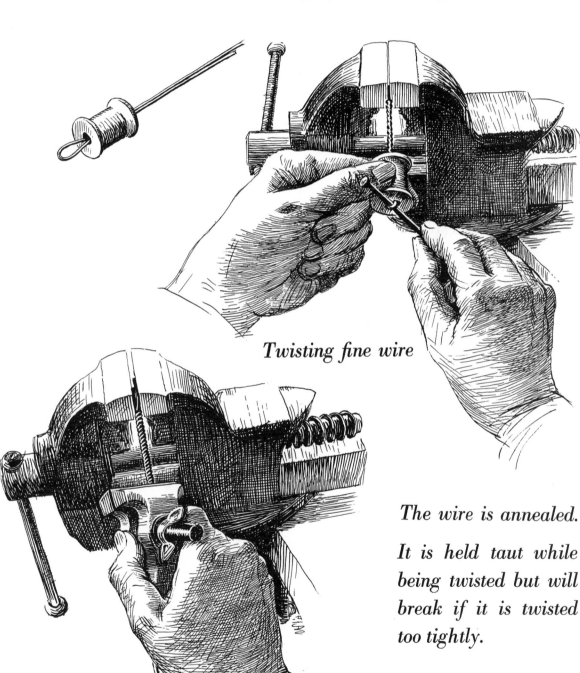

Twisting fine wire

The wire is annealed.

It is held taut while being twisted but will break if it is twisted too tightly.

Twisting heavier wire

Making a round wire coil

Coils of wire can be made on mandrels of various sizes and shapes. The simplest is the coil of round rings made of round wire. There are many uses for the coil. When sawed into rings it may be made into a chain. By pulling the wire on both ends to stretch the coil, an open wavy coil results, which may be curved or bent to follow a line for decoration. The open coil may also be flattened into a decorative band of overlapping rings. A cone shaped coil can be made on a round pointed mandrel (knitting needle). These may be used for pendants to give movement and interest to a design and are sometimes used as a fringe for an edge.

The jig

Select a round steel mandrel the diameter of the coil desired. Place between two blocks of soft wood parallel with the grain of the wood.

Press the blocks between the jaws of the table vise to form a groove in each block. Remove the mandrel from the blocks, and file a groove at a right angle to the groove made by the mandrel.

Coiling the wire

Place the mandrel between the blocks in the groove letting the end extend beyond the blocks about ½ inch.

Hold the blocks in the jaws of the table vise tight enough to hold the blocks but loose enough so the mandrel will turn and move out of the groove as the wire is coiled.

Make a few coils on the end of the mandrel. Clamp the mandrel and coils in the jaws of the hand vise.

Hold the loose end of the wire in the filed groove during the coiling process to guide the wire and to keep the coil even.

Use the hand vise as a handle to turn the mandrel to form the coil.

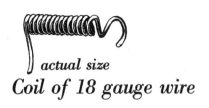

actual size

Coil of 18 gauge wire

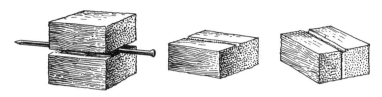

The jig to hold the mandrel

A nail can be used as a mandrel,
  or a knitting needle can be used for a longer coil

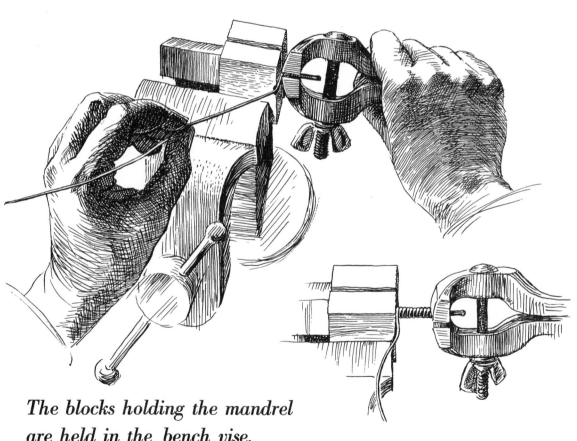

The blocks holding the mandrel
are held in the bench vise.

The protruding end of the mandrel is held in the hand
vise, and the coil is formed by turning the hand vise.

The wire is held taut and is guided by the left hand.

21

Making a flat wire coil

A flat coiled unit is usually made of round wire. It may be the foundation of an article and is often used for decoration, either as a single unit or several combined to make a pattern.

The wire ends of the unit may be turned under at right angles to form staples so that it can be used as a decorative stud on leather or fabric. The unit may hang as a pendant or several may be linked together to form a chain.

The jig

14 gauge or heavier metal sheet. Saw a 1 inch disk or larger.

Drill a hole in the center of the disk the size of the mandrel which determines the size hole in the center of the coil.

File a notch in the edge of the hole the size of the wire to be used for the coil.

Coiling wire 18 gauge or lighter

Cut a wire length, and insert the end and mandrel ½ inch through the hole in the disk, and the wire in the notch.

Bend the annealed wire around the mandrel, and hold both the wire and the mandrel in the jaws of the hand vise. Wind the wire to make the coil by turning the vise.

Keep the coil flat with the thumb of the left hand while coiling. Each ring must touch the ring just made and lie flat on the disk.

Place the hand vise in the jaws of the table vise. Insert the end of the mandrel in the hole of the setting tool. Tap the end of the setting tool to flatten the coil. Repeat this operation often to keep the coil flat.

Coiling wire 16 gauge or heavier

Insert the wire end and mandrel through the hole in the disk. Hold as described above.

Place a hand vise in the jaws of the table vise.

Hold the loose end of the wire in the right hand, and wind on the disk.

The setting tool

Saw a short length of hard wood rod (a broom handle).

File one end smooth and flat and finish with sandpaper.

Drill a hole in the center larger in diameter than the mandrel and deeper than the length of the mandrel.

The jig, p. 17. *Sawing*, p. 8. *Drilling*, p. 10. *Filing*, p. 12.

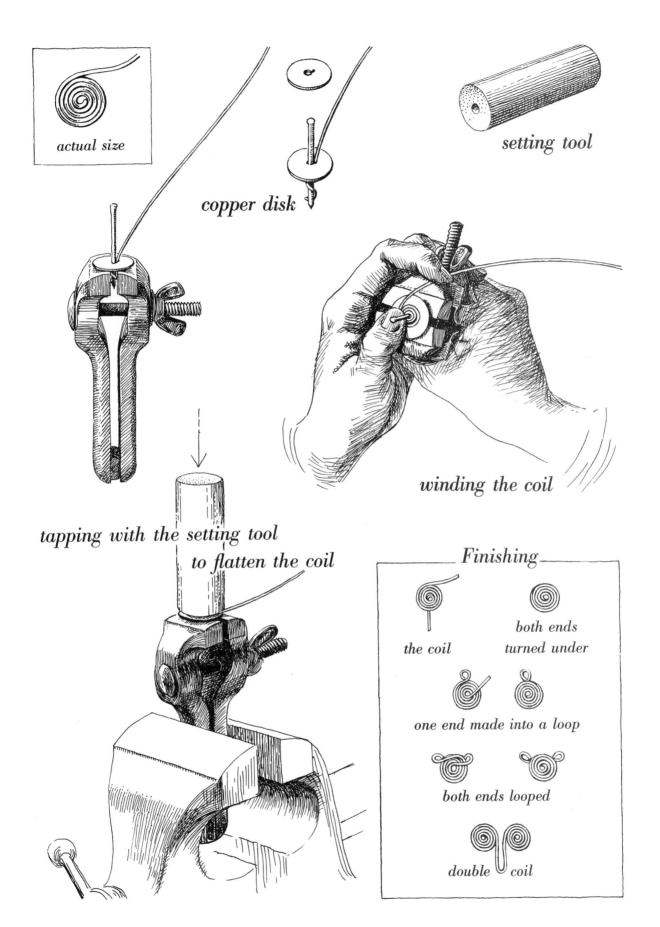

actual size

copper disk

setting tool

winding the coil

tapping with the setting tool
to flatten the coil

Finishing

the coil

both ends
turned under

one end made into a loop

both ends looped

double coil

23

Sawing a coil into links for a chain

Round links combined in various ways for chains

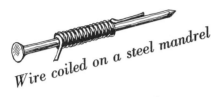

Chain of round rings

Make a round coil of wire.

Insert a wooden core in the coil.

Place the coil in the ring clamp.

Hold the clamp in the jaws of the table vise.

Place a #1 blade in the saw frame and saw the coil into rings.

Hold a ring on each side of the opening with the pliers.

Push the ends beyond each other, then together.

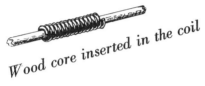

Wire coiled on a steel mandrel

Wood core inserted in the coil

Single chain

Close ⅔ the number required.

Open ⅓ the width of the wire.

Hook the open ring through the two closed rings.

Close the open ring to make an even joint.

Making a round wire coil, p. 20.
Sawing, p. 8.

Opening the rings

right way

wrong way

24

Two chains made from wire units,
and some pendants to hang from
them for necklaces and bracelets

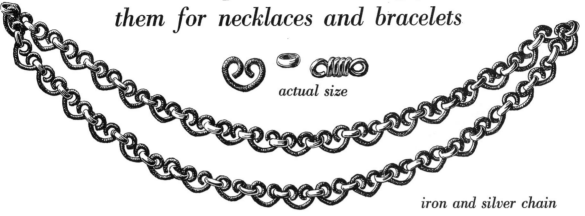

actual size

iron and silver chain

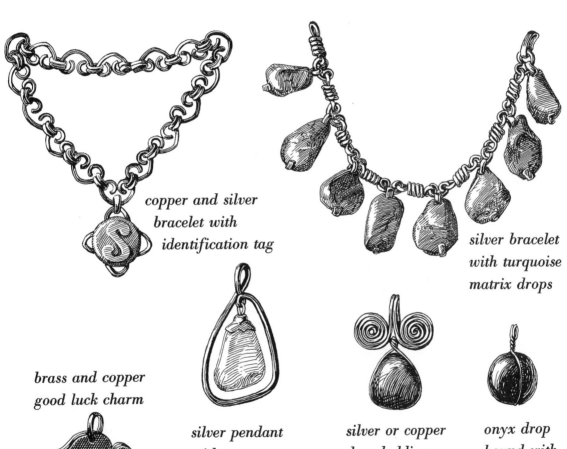

copper and silver
bracelet with
identification tag

silver bracelet
with turquoise
matrix drops

brass and copper
good luck charm

silver pendant
with rose quartz

silver or copper
drop holding
a green stone

onyx drop
bound with
silver wire

The construction of these pieces will
be found on the following pages.

25

a nail

used as a mandrel

Chain of round rings

18 gauge wire

Determine the number of units required for the chain.

Cut a 2½ inch length of wire for each unit.

Coil the wire once around the end of the mandrel.

Hold in the jaws of the table vise.

Coil the wire length around the mandrel by hand.

Remove the coil from the mandrel.

Insert a flat steel tool between the last ring on each end of the coil to make a space. Turn the rings at right angles to the coil with square nose pliers.

Link the units together to form the chain.

Bring the wire ends to the center of the coil with round nose pliers.

Chain of shaped units

18 gauge wire

Place the jig in the jaws of the table vise. Insert a wire end in the hole X.

Bring the wire between 1 and 2. Coil around 1.

Carry the wire to 2 and make a coil. Pull the wire to make the coil tight.

Reverse the position of the coil so the wire in X is pointing up and pull the end to tighten the coil.

Remove the unit from the pegs.

Cut the wire ends where they meet the center wire. Press between the jaws of the square nose pliers, so they lie flat.

Place the unit on 3.

Draw rings together with the tips of the round nose pliers.

Making a round wire coil, p. 20. Linking, p. 24. The jig, p. 17.

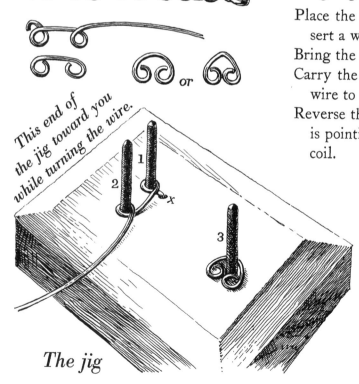

or

This end of the jig toward you while turning the wire.

The jig

26

Identification tag

22 gauge copper sheet 2 inches square

Tin one side.
Saw two ⅝ inch disks.

20 gauge silver sheet ¾ of an inch square

Tin one side.
Transfer the pattern of the initial to the silver.
Saw to pattern.
File all edges smooth. Finish with emery cloth.
Apply flux to the tinned surface.
Place on the untinned side of the copper disk,
   and hold with cotter pins.
Lay on an iron screen with the initial side down
   and place on a hot plate until the solder melts.

18 gauge silver wire

Make four wire units.
Flux the tinned surface of the second disk.
Place the four units on the fluxed surface. Melt
   the solder with the soldering iron, enough to
   hold the units in place.
Flux the tinned surface of the two disks again.
Hold the disks together with cotter pins. Make
   sure the edges of the disks are even and the
   initial is straight with the center loop.
Lay on a screen and hot plate until the solder
   melts. This will show in a bright metallic line
   between the joined edges.
Let the metal cool before removing from the
   screen.

Tinning, p. 14. *Transferring the pattern*, p. 8. *Sawing*,
p. 8. *Filing*, p. 12. *Making wire units*, p. 17. *Soldering*,
p. 14.

front back (tinned)

The initial is soldered to one of the disks

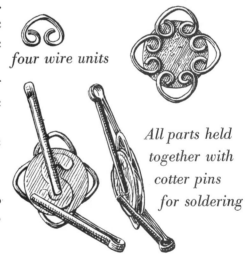

four wire units

All parts held together with cotter pins for soldering

To cap a stone

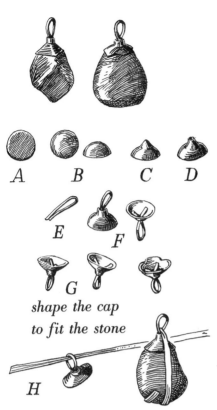

26 gauge silver sheet

Cut and dome a ¼ inch disk A. The size of the disk
    depends upon the stone B.
Place the dome on a lead block with the cup up.
Punch a hole in the center C.
File the rough edge of the hole D.

22 gauge silver wire

Make a loop in a short length of wire E.
Insert the ends through the hole in the dome F.
Spread the wire against the sides of the cup G.
Bend the dome slightly oval to fit the stone.
Insert adhesive tape in the loop.
Apply liquid cement inside the cup.
Bind the dome to the stone to form a cap H.
Remove the tape when the cement is dry.

Disk cutting and punching, p. 40. *Filing*, p. 12.

*shape the cap
to fit the stone*

To bind a stone

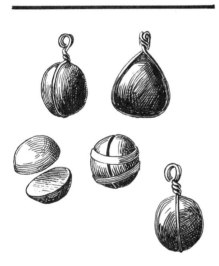

Two identical stones with flat base. Apply liquid
    cement to the base of each. Bind together until
    dry.

22 gauge silver wire

Measure the circumference of the stone.
Cut a length of wire 1 inch longer than measured.
Lay the wire in the groove between the stones.
Twist the wires together, and make a loop.

Mounting a stone with hooks

File a 1/16 inch groove the length of a soft stone.
    Make a notch on each end of the groove.

1/16 inch half round silver wire

Use enough for the length of the stone and the
    hooks. Shape the wire as shown.
Cement the wire into the groove. Bend the ends to
    meet the stone.

Filing, p. 12.

28

Mounting for a stone of irregular shape

Let the wire follow the outline of the stone.
Leave enough space between the stone and wire for movement.
Trace the outline of the stone on a sheet of paper.
Enlarge the traced outline ⅛ inch A.
Measure the outline of the enlarged pattern.
Add 1¾ inches for the working ends and hooks.

14 gauge silver wire

Cut the measured length.
Make a loop on one end of the wire B.
File the other end of wire to measure 18 gauge.
Shape the wire to pattern B.
Cut the extending wire and bend the loop as shown.
Make a loop on the filed end and bring the looped ends together C and solder D.
File edges smooth. Finish with emery cloth.
Cap a stone and hook to the loop.

Filing, p. 12. *Capping a stone*, p. 28. *Flat coil*, p. 22.

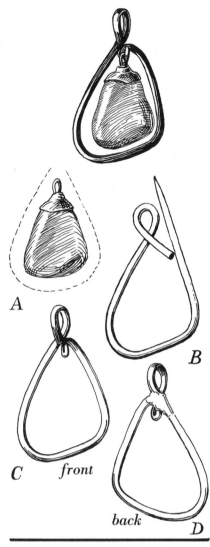

A

B

C   front

back   D

Mounting on which to hang a stone

18 gauge wire 9½ inches

Make a ½ inch coil on each end of the wire.
Make a loop in the center. Turn the loop down to form a hook.

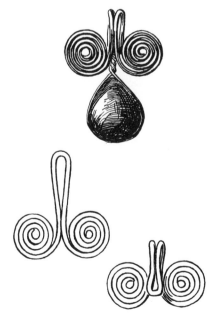

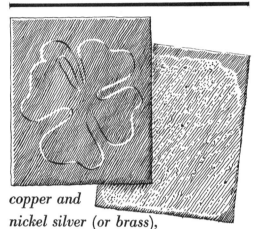

Good luck charm

24 gauge copper sheet 2 inches square

Tin one side.

Trace the design on the untinned side of the sheet.

Saw to pattern.

22 gauge brass 2 inches square

Tin one side.

Flux the tinned surface of both metals.

Hold the metals together with cotter pins.

Place on a screen and hot plate until the solder melts.

When cool wash with pumice powder and a brush.

Saw the brass sheet even with the copper design.

File and emery the edges smooth and even, then polish with a burnisher.

copper and

nickel silver (or brass),

both pieces tinned on one side

Tinning, p. 14. Transferring the pattern, p. 8. Sawing, p. 8. Soldering, p. 14. Filing, p. 12. Burnishing, p. 16.

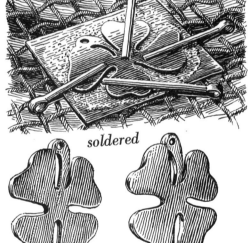

soldered

sawed   *polished*

By following the same procedure other and more personal charms can be made.

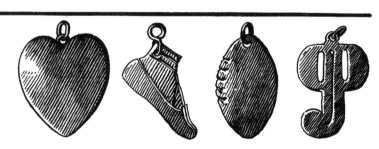

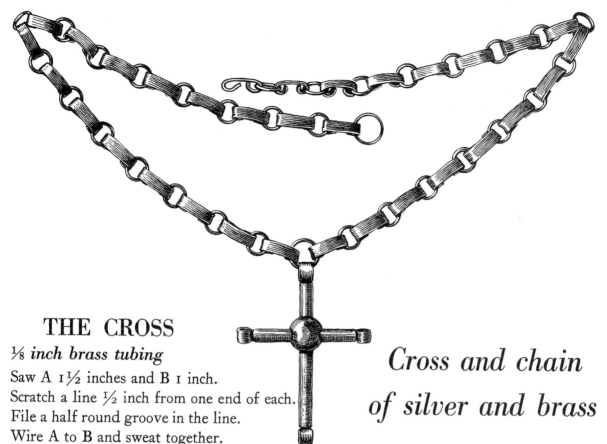

THE CROSS

⅛ inch brass tubing

Saw A 1½ inches and B 1 inch.
Scratch a line ½ inch from one end of each.
File a half round groove in the line.
Wire A to B and sweat together.

22 gauge silver sheet

Saw four ¾ by ⅛ inch strips C.
File C ⅜ inch on one end to fit the tube.
Cut and dome a ⅜ inch disk D.
File the base of the dome to fit the tube.
Tin the filed ends of C and the cup of D.
Insert C in the tubes and hold D on AB with the
    soldering tweezers. Sweat together.
Turn the ends of C on a ⅛ inch mandrel.

THE CHAIN

22 gauge silver sheet

Saw a ⅛ inch strip cut into ¾ inch lengths.
Turn the ends on a 1/16 inch mandrel.

18 gauge brass wire

Make ¼ inch rings for the chain and two ⅜
    inch rings for the cross and clasp.

*Sawing, p. 8. Filing, p. 12. Disk cutting and doming,
p. 40. Tinning, p. 14. Sweating, p. 14. Ring making,
p. 24.*

*Cross and chain
of silver and brass*

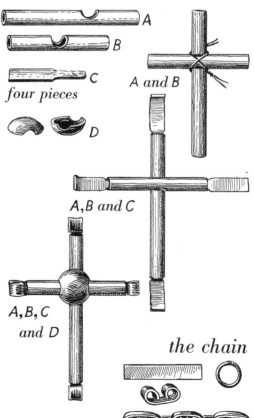

A

B

C
four pieces

D

A and B

A, B and C

*A, B, C
and D*

the chain

Necklace of onyx beads joined by silver links and an onyx pendant

The design was suggested by the marking on the back of the stone, the eye of a fish. Its form and translucent quality lent itself to piercing a fish design. The framework of metal holds the stone. Beads, the same texture and color of the stone, are held together with a silver unit suggesting a sea horse. The mottled edge of orange and brown of the stone is repeated in the eye and again in the beads. The luster of the silver gives good color and brilliance to the finished piece. Other translucent stones suitable for jewelry are often found which will suggest many designs.

THE PENDANT

Draw the outline of the stone on a sheet of paper and add prongs to the outline at the top, bottom and sides.

Place the fish design within the outline so the marking on the stone will be in position for the eye of the fish. The pierced design must be in the frame which holds the base of the stone.

22 gauge silver sheet

Transfer the pattern to the silver.

Drill a hole in the section to be pierced.

Pierce the design, and saw the outline of the pattern.

File all edges even. Finish with emery cloth.

Polish with tripoli and a felt buff.

Place the stone in position on the metal. Turn the metal which extends beyond the edge of the stone with round nose pliers to hold the stone firmly. Round any sharp corners with a file.

Remove scratches and polish with a burnisher.

Transferring the pattern, p. 8. Drilling, p. 10. Piercing, p. 10. Filing, p. 12. Cleaning, p. 16. Burnishing, p. 16.

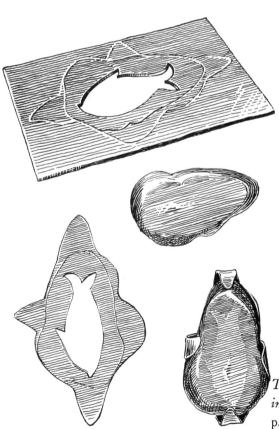

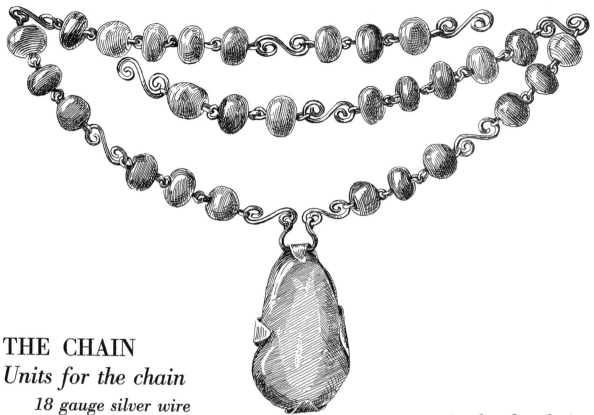

THE CHAIN
Units for the chain
18 gauge silver wire

Cut a wire length 1½ inches A.

Make a ring on each end of the wire.

Loop the wire in the center, and flatten to hold the hook of the pendant. Bring the rings almost together.

Cut ten lengths of wire 1½ inches.

Coil the wire with round nose pliers B.

Cut twenty-eight lengths of wire ¾ inch C.

Make a ring on one end of each wire.

Assembling the chain

Hook one ring of A into a coiled end of B.

Hook C into the other B coil.

Insert the stem of C through the hole in the bead, and a B coil.

Turn the stem of C to form a ring. The bead should be held tight by the C rings.

Continue joining the wire units and beads until half of the chain has been finished.

Repeat the above to complete the chain.

Hook the pendant in A.

Ring making, p. 24. *Chain making,* p. 24.

units for the chain

assembling the chain

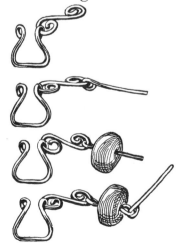

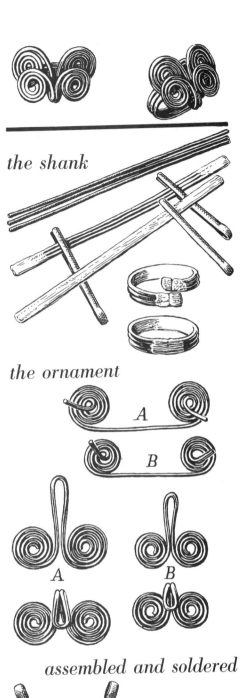

the shank

the ornament

A

B

A   B

assembled and soldered

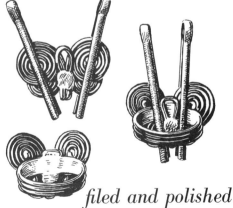

filed and polished

Ring of flat coils

Ring shank

18 gauge silver wire

Measure the finger with ring sizes. The ring shown is a 5½ ring size.

Cut three lengths of wire 2½ inches long.

Solder the wires together on the ends ¼ inch to hold them even.

Solder the three lengths together.

File and smooth with emery cloth.

Shape around the ring mandrel on size #6 (a half size larger than the finished ring) with the solder on the inside of the ring.

Saw the wires where they overlap.

Join the ends and solder together.

Ornament

Cut two lengths of wire, one 8 inches long and one 6 inches long.

Make flat coils on the ends of A and B with holding ends in the jig ¼ inch. Wind the coils toward each other and the holding ends on the same side. Cut the holding ends.

Loop the center of A and B on a 1/16 inch mandrel, with the coils on the outside.

Unit A should measure 1 inch by 1 inch, and B ¾ inch by ¾ inch.

Turn A loop ⅜ inch, and B loop ¼ inch.

Insert B through A, press together between square nose pliers so they lie flat. Solder together.

Hook AB over the joint of the shank and solder together.

Turn the looped end toward the coils.

File the inside smooth and finish with emery.

Soldering, p. 14. *Filing*, p. 12. *Sawing*, p. 8. *Making a flat coil*, p. 22.

34

Necklace of flat coils

The coiled units

18 gauge wire

Cut twenty wire lengths 6 inches.

Make twenty flat coils, winding the wire five times to
    make the unit. Leave ⅜ inch wire end on each
    unit A.

Let ½ inch of the outside wire rest on the back of the
    coil. Bend flat against the coil B.

Cut the wire ⅜ inch from the edge of the coil to the
    end of the wire.

Make a ⅛ inch ring on the other wire end C.

Join the coiled units with ¼ inch rings to make the
    chain D.

The catch

Cut a wire length 3 inches.

Bend in the center and bring the ends together.

Make a hook on the looped end and a ring on each wire
    end.

Link to one end of the chain. To fasten, hook the catch
    to the last ring on the other end of the chain.

Making a flat coil, p. 22. *Ring making*, p. 24. *Linking*, p. 24.

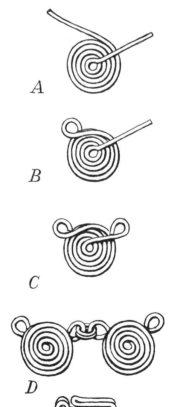

A

B

C

D

E

35

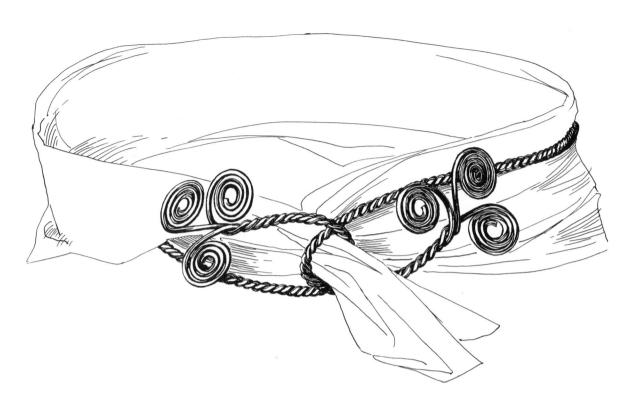

Scarf holder
of coiled and twisted wire

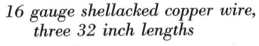

16 gauge shellacked copper wire,
  three 32 inch lengths

Remove all kinks.

Clamp 4 inches of the three ends in the jaws of
  the table vise.

Hold 4 inches of the other ends in the jaws of
  the hand vise.

Pull the wires so they are taut and even.

Give the hand vise sixty full turns to twist the
  wire.

Make six flat coils on the wire ends.

Removing kinks, p. 17. *Twisting wire,* p. 18. *Making
a flat coil,* p. 22.

36

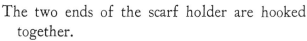

The two ends of the scarf holder are hooked
   together.
A scarf is folded around the wire twist at the
   back and brought to the front. Knot the ends
   together to hold the wire loops in place.

*The same process is used in
making the scarf holder
and bracelet, the difference
being the length of the
wires, the number of turns
and the final shaping.*

Bracelet
of twisted and
coiled wire

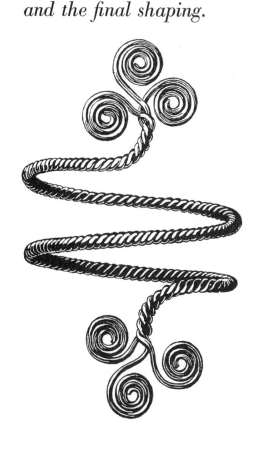

The bracelet is constructed in the same
way as the scarf holder. The wires may
be cut longer or shorter depending upon
the number of times the wire coils
around the arm.

Twist and coil the wire. Follow instructions on page 36 (scarf holder).
Form the bracelet around the head of a
   wooden mallet.
Spread and taper slightly to fit the arm.

Wire twisting, p. 18. *Making a flat coil,*
p. 22.

Barrette
of flat coils

Coils

18 gauge silver wire

Cut six lengths of wire 8 inches.

Make a flat coil on the ends.

Loop the center and bring the coils together and hook into each other.

Cut one length of wire 4 inches.

Coil one end, leave a ½ inch length to insert between the last two double coils.

Tap the loops flat on the coils.

Solder the loops together with the soldering iron. Adjust the coils to overlap with the stems close together. Bend to a slight curve.

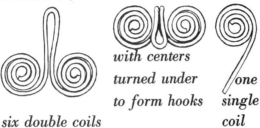

with centers turned under to form hooks

six double coils

one single coil

The clasp

The clasp is commercial, and should be narrow enough to be covered by the coils and long enough to support the coils.

Tin the top of the clasp. Flux the tinned surface of the clasp and the loops on the back. Hold firmly with cotter pins and sweat together.

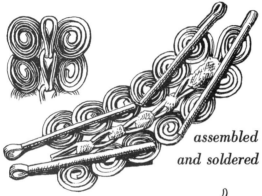

assembled and soldered

Making a flat coil, p. 22. Soldering, p. 14. Tinning, p. 14. Sweating, p. 14.

Terminal ornament

Cut a wire length 1½ inches and make a ring on each end.

Place a small piece of pure tin in each ring.

Melt into a ball with the tip of the soldering iron. A ⅛ inch silver bead may be inserted on the wire ends and soldered.

Loop the wire in the center.

File a ¼ inch silver bead to fit on the first loop of the coils.

Insert the looped end of the wire through the hole in the bead and solder together.

Cut the loop and spread the wires.

Fit the filed bead over the looped end.

Solder the bead and wires to the coils.

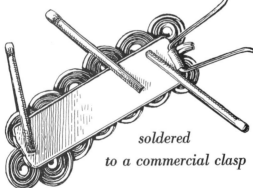

soldered to a commercial clasp

Terminal ornament

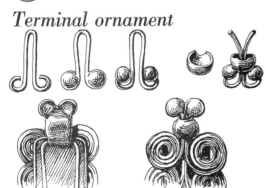

Filing, p. 12. Soldering, p. 14. Making a flat coil, p. 22.

Band bracelet with dangles

18 gauge copper sheet

Cut a strip of copper 5½ inches by ½ inch.
Scratch a line lengthwise through the center.

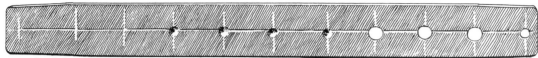

marked by the dividers, marked by the center punch,   holes drilled

Center punch and drill nine ⅛ inch holes on the
  line and two 1/16 inch holes on each end.
Bend to form the bracelet. Polish and lacquer.

1/16 half round silver wire

Cut a 7 inch length.
Hook through the holes in the end of the bracelet.

1/16 flat silver wire

Cut nine 1½ inch lengths.
Bend each piece in the center. Insert the wire
  ends from the front over the silver wire and
  through the ⅛ inch holes.
Bend and hook over the edges of the band.

18 gauge copper wire

Cut nine 5½ inch lengths.
Make flat coils of wire. Polish and lacquer.
Cut fifteen 1 inch lengths of wire.
Make a ¼ inch loop on the end of each wire.
Thread nine of the wires with ¼ inch silver
  beads.
Thread six of the wires through the 3/16 inch
  silver beads and loop the wire ends.
Hook the smaller beads through the end loops
  (three at each end) and hook the larger beads
  to the hooks on one edge of the bracelet and
  the coils to the hooks on the other edge.

*Center punching, p. 10. Drilling, p. 10. Polishing,
p. 16. Lacquering, p. 16. Making a flat coil, p. 22.*

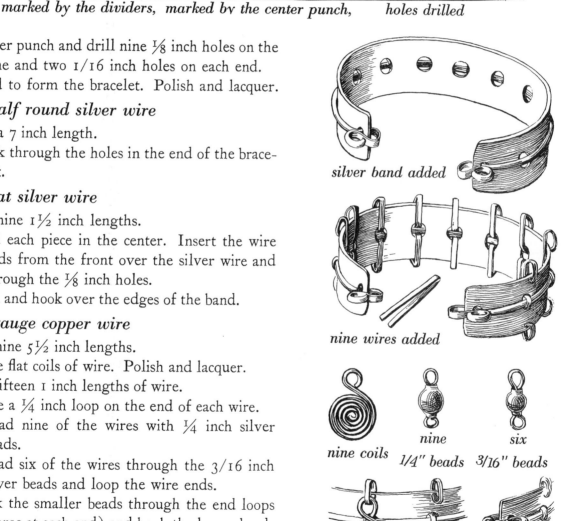

silver band added

nine wires added

nine coils   nine   six
*   1/4" beads   3/16" beads*

beads and coils added

Making Disks and Domes

Disks and domes are used as the foundation of jewelry and also as a means of decoration. They are often given a high polish and take the place of stones in a design. Sometimes wire units are applied to a flat disk or a dome surface for variety and texture.

Cutting disks

20 gauge or lighter sheet metal
Lay the metal on a lead block.
Cut a disk from the metal sheet with a dapping die cutter.

18 gauge or heavier sheet metal
Make a circle with the dividers on the metal.
Saw or cut the disk. This applies also to oversize disks.

Punching domes

Select a hollow in the dapping die block slightly larger than the disk. Raise the disk with the dapping die punch to make the dome. Raise domes larger than the standard punches with the round head of a steel hammer or mallet. Place a disk too large for the dapping die block in a hollow made in a lead or wooden block and dome the disk with the round head of the mallet. To smooth the larger domes, place the mallet head in the jaws of the table vise, the round end up. Hold the cup side of the dome on the mallet. Hammer the domed surface with a mallet to make it smooth.

Sawing, p. 8.

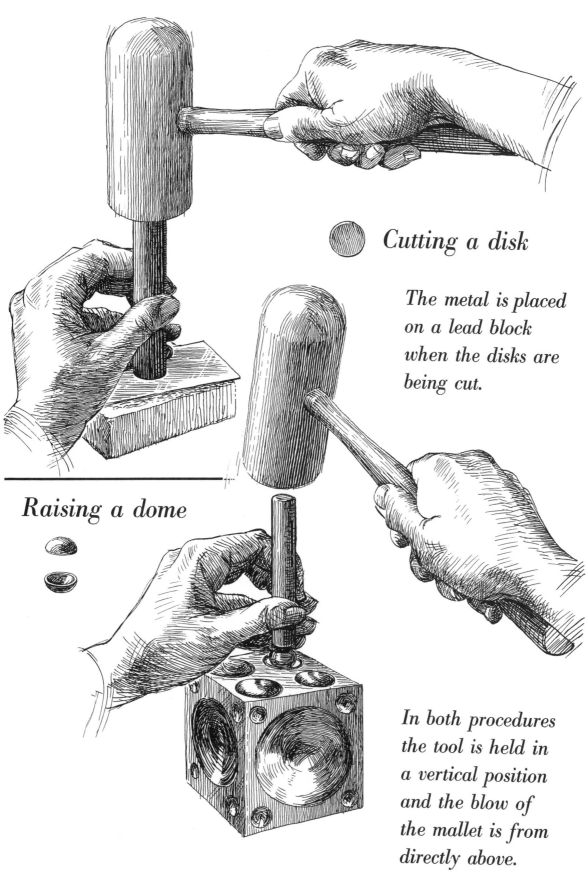

Cutting a disk

The metal is placed
on a lead block
when the disks are
being cut.

Raising a dome

In both procedures
the tool is held in
a vertical position
and the blow of
the mallet is from
directly above.

Necklace of disks and domes
Disk and dome unit

22 gauge silver sheet

Cut ten ⅝ inch disks with the dapping die cutter.

Draw a line through the center of each disk A.

Measure 1/16 inch from the edge and indicate with a scratch on the centered line.

Scratch a center line on one side of a 5/16 inch dapping die cutter B.

Register the line on A with the line on B and cut out a disk.

Dome the small disk and file the top of the dome, C.

22 gauge silver wire

Cut a wire length 1¼ inches.

Make a ⅛ inch ring on one end of the wire D.

Solder the ring on the filed section of the dome E.

Loop the wire end around the small rim of the disk, then around a mandrel to form a coil. Turn the wire end inside the coil.

The chain

Hammer two wire nails ½ inch apart into a block of wood to make a jig.

Cut off the nail heads and file smooth.

22 gauge silver wire

Make an oval coil of wire on the jig.

Remove the coil from the jig and insert a piece of cardboard through the coil to keep it straight while sawing.

Saw the coil on one side to form oval rings.

Bring the wire ends together and solder the joint.

Hold the center firmly together with the pliers.

Insert the end of the round nose pliers in one looped end and turn forward. Repeat with the other looped end and turn backward.

Join, with a ring, the looped ends of the two oval links and the coil on the disk.

Repeat the above to form the chain.

Disk cutting and punching, p. 40. *Soldering*, p. 14. *Sawing*, p. 8. *Ring making*, p. 24. *Linking*, p. 24.

A

B

D

E

C

*Two simple chains, either
of which can be used*

or

back   front

*or the drop can be
this shape*

A good way to hold the dome firm while soldering.

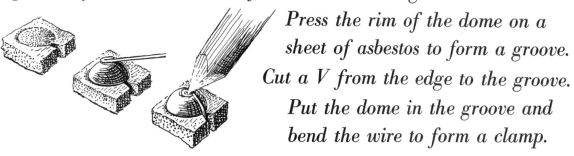

Press the rim of the dome on a
sheet of asbestos to form a groove.
Cut a V from the edge to the groove.
Put the dome in the groove and
bend the wire to form a clamp.

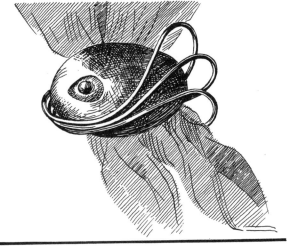

Scarf holder

22 gauge copper sheet

Cut the metal to pattern A.

Pierce the opening.

File all edges and finish with emery cloth.

Dome A slightly. Tin the cupped side.

24 gauge brass sheet

Cut and dome a ⅜ inch disk B. File the base even.

Punch a hole in the center.

24 gauge silver sheet

Cut and dome a ⅛ inch disk.

22 gauge silver wire

Cut and double a 1½ inch length.

Solder the looped end in the cup of the small dome C.

Insert the wire ends through the hole on the cup side in B.

Make a coil on each wire end.

Solder B and the coils to the back of A.

18 gauge silver wire

Cut three 4 inch lengths.

Solder the ends together D.

Cut one 3 inch length E.

Shape and tin the coiled end.

Hold D and E to A with cotter pins.

Solder all together.

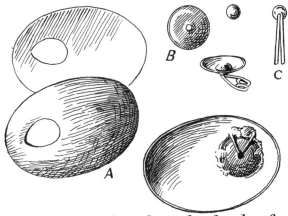

B and C soldered to the back of A

Piercing, p. 10. *Filing*, p. 12. *Disk cutting and punching*, p. 40. *Making a flat coil*, p. 22. *Soldering*, p. 14.

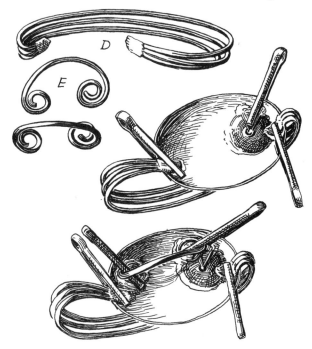

the wires, D and E, soldered to A

Belt buckle and buttons

20 gauge copper sheet

Cut and dome two 1½ inch disks A for the buckle, and as many disks A as desired for buttons.

26 gauge brass sheet

Tin the sheet. Cut to pattern B.
Dome B to fit the A domes.

22 gauge copper sheet

Cut two strips ¾ by ¼ inch C.
Turn the ends to fit inside A.
Cut a strip 1 inch by ¼ inch D.
Turn one end to form a hook.

18 gauge copper wire

Cut the required number of 2 inch wire lengths for the button shanks and one length for the buckle fastener.

Bend E for the button shanks and F for the buckle fastener.

Tin C, D, E and F where the contact is made with A domes.

Flux the cupped side of B.

Hold to A with cotter pins. Place on screen and hot plate until the solder melts.

Flux C, D and F and hold with cotter pins on the cupped side of the large A domes.

Make sure B is held firmly on the domed side.

Sweat together. Solder E on the back of the small A domes with the soldering iron.

Disk cutting and punching, p. 40. *Tinning*, p. 14. *Sweating*, p. 14. *Soldering*, p. 14.

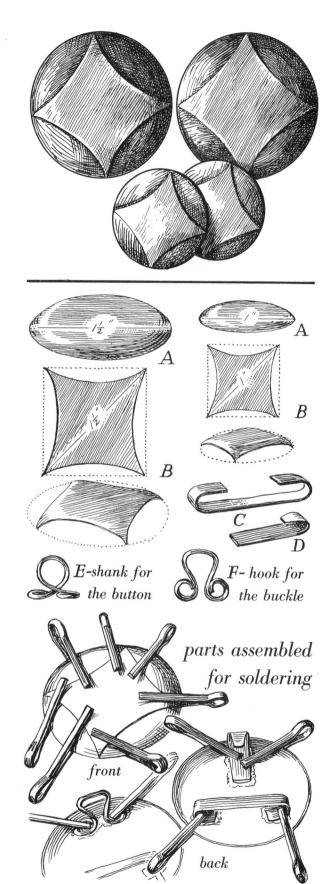

A

A

B

B

C

D

E-shank for the button

F- hook for the buckle

parts assembled for soldering

front

back

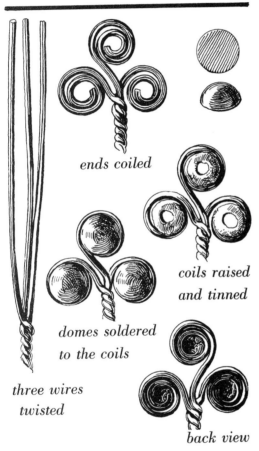

Bracelet
of twisted wire
with domes

14 gauge copper wire

Cut three 15 inch lengths of wire.

Hold 3 inches of the ends in the jaws of the table vise.

Clamp 3 inches of the other loose ends in the jaws of the hand vise.

Hold taut and give the hand vise twenty-four full turns.

Make a flat wire coil on each wire end.

Cut the ¼ inch holding end even with the coil.

Raise the center of the coil on a lead block with a dapping die punch and tin the raised center.

24 gauge silver sheet

Cut and dome six ⅜ inch disks.

File the base of the domes even.

Tin the inside of the domes.

Flux the tinned surface of the domes and coils.

Lay one of the coil ends on the screen and hot plate.

Place a dome on each coil and solder together.

Repeat the above process on the other end.

Hold the head of a wooden mallet in the jaws of the table vise.

Bend the twisted wire length around the mallet to form the bracelet. Shape to fit the arm.

Curve one end with round nose pliers. Bend the other end. The coils must lie flat on the arm.

22 gauge silver wire

Cut three 15 inch lengths.

Wind a wire in the first groove of the twist.

Leave one inch of the wire free on each end.

Coil the silver wire in every third groove between the copper wires.

Pull the wire tight during the coiling process.

Repeat the above with the other wire lengths.

ends coiled

coils raised and tinned

domes soldered to the coils

three wires twisted

back view

silver wires added

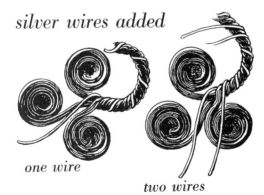

one wire

two wires

Wire twisting, p. 18. *Making a flat coil*, p. 22. *Filing*, p. 12. *Disk cutting and punching*, p. 40. *Tinning*, p. 14. *Soldering*, p. 14.

Coil the loose ends.

Solder the coils on the back under the domes.

Smooth any rough surfaces with a file and emery cloth.

Rub the domes with fine pumice powder to remove scratches.

Polish with metal polish. Finish with chamois skin.

Lacquer the twisted wire.

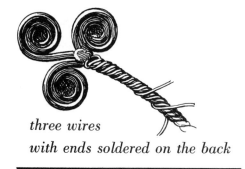

three wires
with ends soldered on the back

Ring ornamented with a dome

14 gauge silver wire

Cut one 8 inch length of wire.

Make a ½ inch flat coil on one end.

Cut the ¼ inch holding wire.

Tap the coil flat with a mallet and raise the center with a dapping die punch. Tin the raised center.

24 gauge silver sheet

Cut and dome a ⅜ inch disk.

Tin the inside of the dome.

Place the coiled end on the screen and the dome on the tinned coil. Sweat together.

Hold the coil on the #3 ring on the ring mandrel and coil the loose end of the wire to form the ring.

Curve the ends and solder a ¼ inch silver bead on the wire end with tin solder and a soldering iron.

Cut and dome a ⅛ inch disk and solder to cover the hole in the bead.

Making a flat coil, p. 22. Disk cutting and punching, p. 40. Tinning, p. 14. Soldering, p. 14. Polishing, p. 16. Lacquering, p. 16.

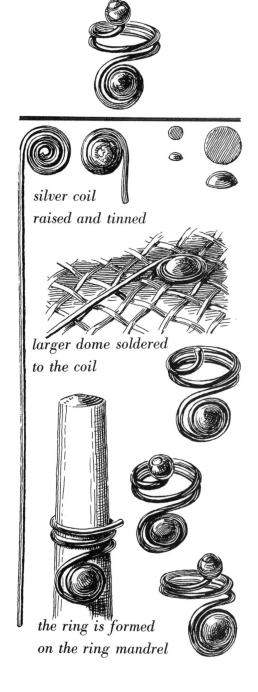

silver coil
raised and tinned

larger dome soldered
to the coil

the ring is formed
on the ring mandrel

Slide for a sport tie

20 gauge copper sheet — turquoise matrix stone

Transfer the patterns A and B to the copper sheet. Cut both to pattern.

Place B in the forming block and curve slightly.

Place the stone on A and indicate the edge of the stone with a scratch line on each arm. Remove the stone and turn the ends at right angles on the scratched lines.

Tin the back of A and hold on the curved surface of B with cotter pins.

Place on a screen and hot plate until the solder melts.

20 gauge copper wire — woven silk cord

Make two tapered coils C about seven rings each. The small end of the coil should fit the cord snugly.

Hold the coils together with cotter pins and solder together. Leave a thin coat of solder on the back.

Solder C to the back of B. Make sure the soldering tweezers hold A on the front while holding C on the back.

Place on a screen and hot plate until the solder melts.

Make two tapered coils about fifteen rings each D. A knitting needle may be used for the mandrel.

Remove all scratches with pumice powder and emery cloth.

Set the stone between the arms of A. Turn the ends over the stone with the burnisher.

Polish and lacquer the slide B and the coils C and D.

Wind the cord ends with fine binding wire.

Cover the ends with liquid cement and insert in the coils D.

To make the forming block

Drill a ¾ inch hole in a block of wood.

Saw the block in half to divide the hole lengthwise.

File the curve of the groove to an oval shape. Smooth with sandpaper.

File and smooth a dowel or broom handle to fit the curve in the block.

Transferring the pattern, p. 8. *Tinning*, p. 14. *Soldering*, p. 14. *Making a tapered coil*, p. 20. *Burnishing*, p. 16. *Polishing*, p. 16. *Lacquering*, p. 16.

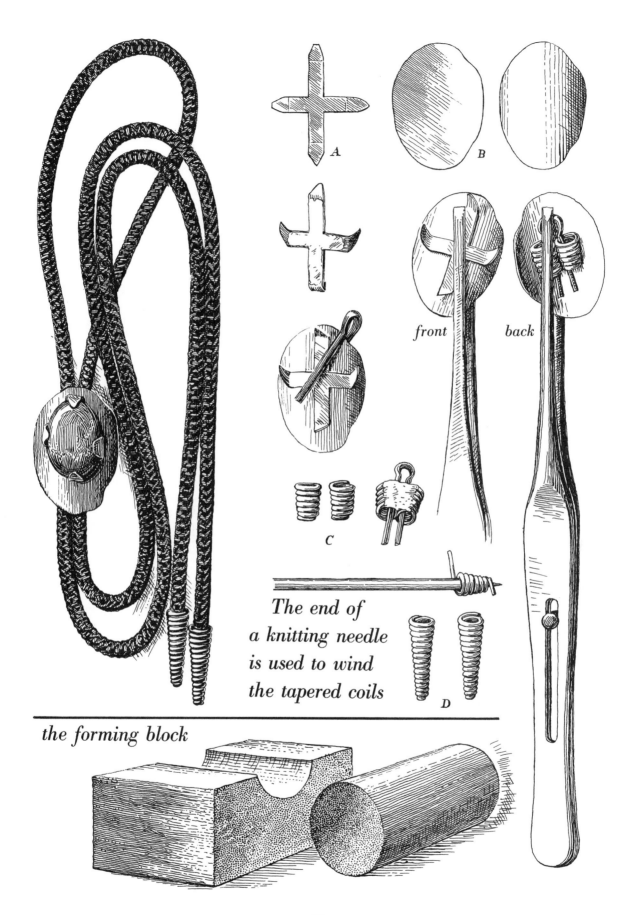

A

B

front   back

C

The end of
a knitting needle
is used to wind
the tapered coils

D

the forming block

49

paper pattern

silver, shaped and marked

holes drilled, prongs marked

prongs cut and finished

bead soldered to the cup

Pendant with reflected stone

The stone in this pendant is chrysocola with a high polish, the bright color reflecting on the polished surface of the silver cup. Any stone with a flat base can be used. The pendant hangs from a cord which matches the blue of the stone.

24 gauge silver sheet

Cut a paper pattern larger than the base of the stone.

Transfer the pattern to the silver and cut out.

Scratch the outline of the stone in the center.

Dome on a lead block with a round headed wooden mallet.

Hold the cup side on the round head of a wooden mallet held in the jaws of the table vise.

Tap the surface with a flat faced steel hammer.

Flatten the dome to fit the base of the stone.

Center punch inside the outline of the stone.

Drill holes as indicated. Saw four prongs.

Turn the prongs up from the cup.

Round the end of the prongs with a file.

Tape a ¼ inch silver bead on a wooden stick.

File a slit in the bead.

Insert the pointed end of the cup in the slit.

Solder to the bead on the back with tin solder.

50

Bowknot barrette

22 gauge silver sheet

Transfer the design to the metal.

Cut A and B to pattern.

Cut a strip ½ inch by 3/16 inch C.

Cut a strip ¼ inch by ¾ inch D.

File all edges smooth.

Bend A and B slightly.

Bend C at right angles to fit the center of B.

Make hooks on both ends of D.

File the curve of the hooks flat.

Tin the filed surface of the hooks and the flat top of D, also the top of the commercial clasp.

Solder D to the tinned surface of the clasp.

Place A on B and C in the center.

Bend the arms of C around AB as shown.

Solder C to B.

Place the tinned hooks of D on the back of B.

Solder in place with the soldering iron.

Transferring the pattern, p. 8. *Filing,* p. 12. *Tinning,* p. 14. *Soldering,* p. 14.

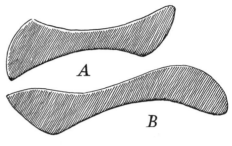

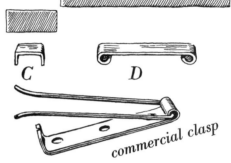

C   D

commercial clasp

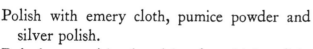

D soldered to the clasp

Polish with emery cloth, pumice powder and silver polish.

Rub the cup with a burnisher for a high polish.

Bend the prongs over the stone with a burnisher.

Insert the cord through the bead on the pendant.

String the beads on the cord, holding in place with a knot.

Transferring the pattern, p. 8. *Doming,* p. 10. *Removing scratches,* p. 16. *Filing,* p. 12. *Burnishing,* p. 16. *Polishing,* p. 16.

C soldered to A and B, back view

all parts soldered together,

side view

Boy's ring
of silver and onyx

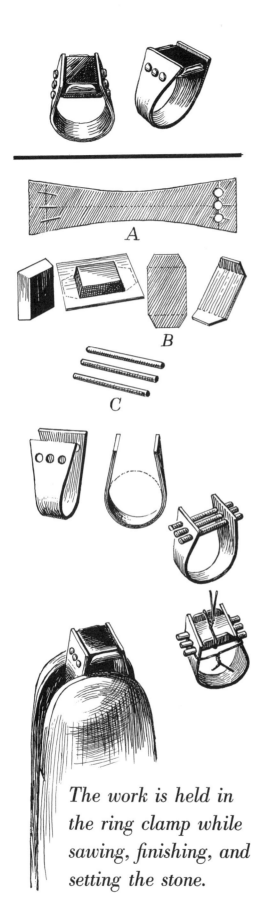

The work is held in the ring clamp while sawing, finishing, and setting the stone.

The depth of the stone determines the length of the ring shank and also the distance the holes are bored from the ends. The stone may be oblong or square, with or without a beveled edge.

Measure the finger with ring sizes, and the circumference of the size on the ring gauge. Draw the pattern for the shank, allowing for enough metal to extend above the stone.

18 gauge silver sheet

Transfer the pattern and saw the ring shank A.
Place one arm of the dividers over the end of A and set to measure ⅛ inch more than the depth of the stone, scratch a line.
Repeat on the other end.
Divide these lines into three parts.
Drill holes, as marked, to fit 12 gauge wire.

Oblong stone ⅛ inch in depth

Measure the base of the stone and add ⅛ inch to the length on each end.

26 gauge silver sheet

Transfer the pattern B to the metal.
Cut B and bend the ends. Tin the back.

12 gauge silver wire

Cut three lengths ¾ inch C.
Tin the wires on one side.
Bend A around the ring mandrel to make a loop.
Thread wires C through the holes. Be sure the tinned side of the wire is turned up.
Flux and bind B to the wires.
Bind the arms of A close to the edge of B.
Place on a screen and hot plate until the solder melts.
Hold in a ring clamp. Saw the protruding wires leaving a short end. File to form knobs.
Place the stone in B. Bend and burnish the silver over the stone. Burnish the ends of A.

Transferring the pattern, p. 8. Sawing, p. 8. Drilling, p. 10. Tinning, p. 14. Soldering, p. 14. Burnishing, p. 16.

Girl's ring of silver and chrysocola

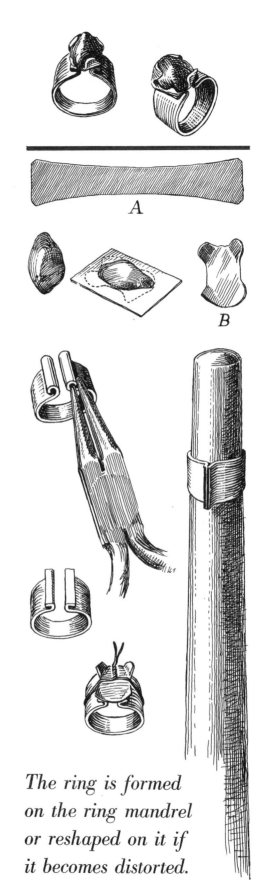

The width of the stone determines the length of the shank. Measure the finger with ring sizes, and determine the circumference of the ring on the ring gauge. Draw the pattern of the shank long enough to include the circumference of the ring and the two flanges.

18 gauge silver sheet

Transfer the pattern for the ring shank to the metal A.

Saw to pattern. File all edges smooth.

22 gauge silver sheet

Draw the outline of the stone on a sheet of paper and add enough to the outline to form arms to hold the stone.

Transfer the pattern to the metal. Saw to pattern B.

Bend the arms at right angles and file them to the thickness of 26 gauge.

Bend A around the ring mandrel. Shape with a mallet.

Turn the ends with pliers and tap to flatten slightly.

File across the turned ends to make flat and even.

Tin the underside of B and the turned ends of A.

Flux the tinned surface of A and B. Wire together.

Place on a screen and hot plate until the solder melts.

Clean and polish.

Place the stone on B. Bend and burnish the arms over the stone. File any rough edges and smooth with emery cloth. Burnish to a high polish.

Transferring the pattern, p. 8. *Filing*, p. 12. *Tinning*, p. 14. *Polishing*, p. 16. *Burnishing*, p. 16.

The ring is formed on the ring mandrel or reshaped on it if it becomes distorted.

Butterfly brooch of copper and brass

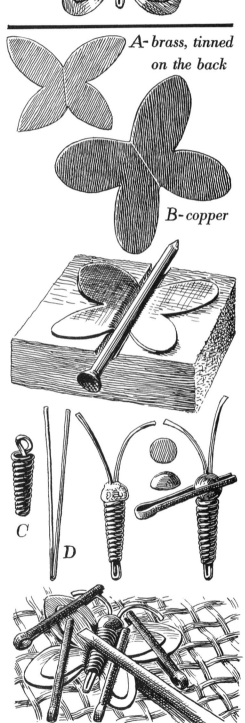

A- brass, tinned on the back

B- copper

C

D

28 gauge brass sheet

Saw A from the brass sheet which has been tinned on one side.

22 gauge copper sheet

Saw B from the copper sheet.

File all edges smooth and finish with emery cloth.

Make a groove in a wooden block.

Draw a center line through A and B.

Place the tinned side of A on the block and hammer into the groove.

Hammer a groove in B. File and tin the rib on the back resulting from the groove on the front.

18 gauge copper wire

Cut a 6 inch length of wire.

Make a ½ inch tapered coil 3/16 to ⅛ inch C.

Bend the beginning ring at right angles to the coil.

Tin one side of the coil.

Cut a 3½ inch length. Loop in the center D.

Insert the looped end through the ring into the coil.

Solder the wire to the ring.

26 gauge copper sheet

Cut and dome a ¼ inch disk.

Solder the dome to the coil.

Flux the tinned surface of A and C.

Hold together with cotter pins and soldering tweezers.

Place on a screen and hot plate until the solder melts.

Tin the back of a commercial clasp. Solder to the tinned surface of B with a soldering iron.

Polish and finish with lacquer.

Sawing, p. 8. *Filing,* p. 10. *Tinning,* p. 14. *Soldering,* p. 14. *Polishing,* p. 16. *Making a tapered coil,* p. 20.

Butterfly brooch
of silver

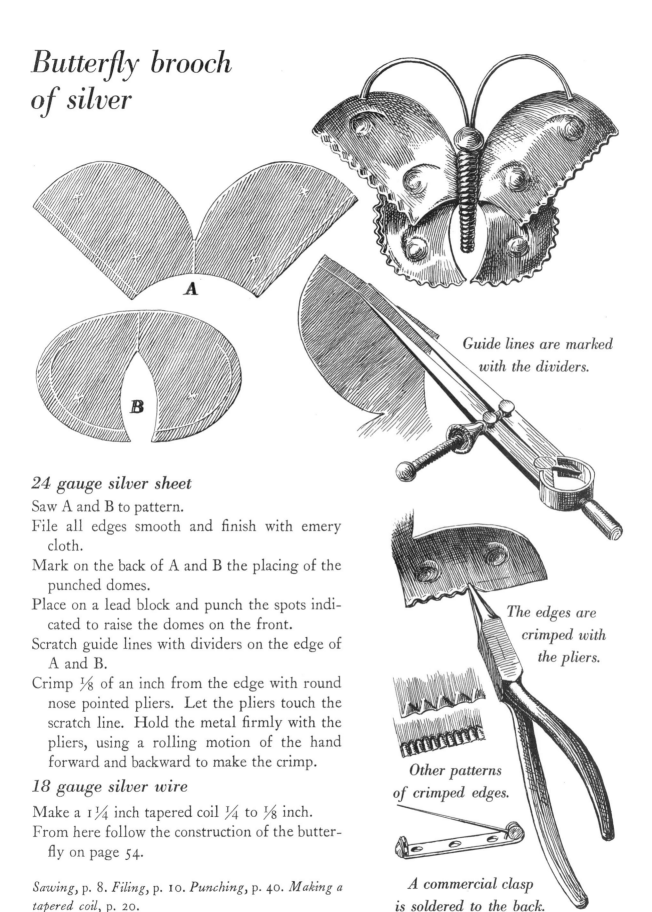

Guide lines are marked
with the dividers.

24 gauge silver sheet

Saw A and B to pattern.

File all edges smooth and finish with emery
cloth.

Mark on the back of A and B the placing of the
punched domes.

Place on a lead block and punch the spots indicated to raise the domes on the front.

Scratch guide lines with dividers on the edge of
A and B.

Crimp ⅛ of an inch from the edge with round
nose pointed pliers. Let the pliers touch the
scratch line. Hold the metal firmly with the
pliers, using a rolling motion of the hand
forward and backward to make the crimp.

18 gauge silver wire

Make a 1¼ inch tapered coil ¼ to ⅛ inch.

From here follow the construction of the butter-
fly on page 54.

Sawing, p. 8. *Filing*, p. 10. *Punching*, p. 40. *Making a
tapered coil*, p. 20.

The edges are
crimped with
the pliers.

Other patterns
of crimped edges.

A commercial clasp
is soldered to the back.

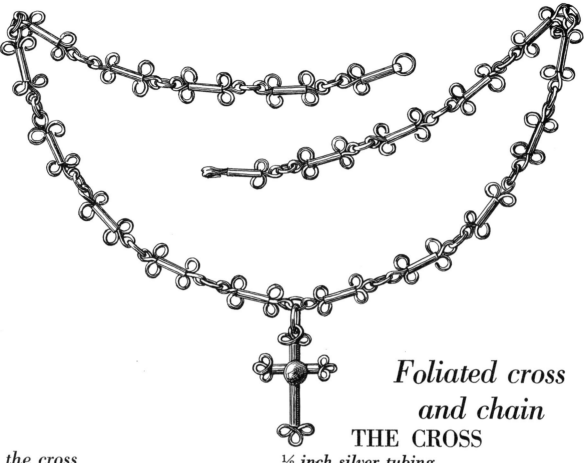

the cross

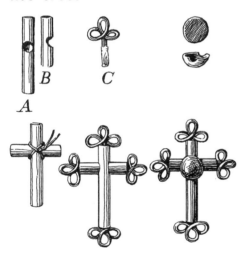

A   *B*   *C*

the chain

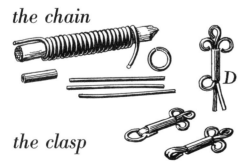

D

the clasp

Foliated cross and chain
THE CROSS

⅛ inch silver tubing

Saw A ¾ inch and B ½ inch.

20 gauge brass wire

Cut four 1 inch lengths and make units C.

24 gauge silver sheet

Cut and dome a 3/16 inch disk.

Directions for making the cross are on page 31.

THE CHAIN

⅛ inch silver tubing

Saw the required number of 5/16 inch lengths.

20 gauge brass wire

Cut three 1 inch lengths for each tube.

Insert the wires in the tubes letting them extend ⅜ inch from each end. Coil the ends D.

Link the D units together with ⅛ inch rings.

Make hooks on two of the units and solder a ring in one hook.

Making coiled units, p. 17. Disk cutting and punching, p. 40. Tinning, p. 14. Soldering, p. 14.

56

Chain with onyx and silver beads

26 gauge sheet brass

Cut and dome two ½ inch disks for each onyx bead in the chain.

Lay the dome, cup up, on a lead block. Punch a hole in the center of each.

File the rough edges smooth and finish with emery cloth.

Coat the inside of the domes with liquid cement and place on a ¼ inch onyx bead. The holes in the bead and domes must register. Let the cement dry.

20 gauge brass wire

Cut two lengths 1¼ inches and one length 1½ inches, three wires for each onyx bead. Make a hook on one end of each wire.

Insert two short wires and one longer wire through the hole in the capped onyx bead, being sure the long wire is in the center between the short wires. Turn the ends to hold the bead firmly.

Make a ⅛ inch wire coil. Saw the coil into rings.

Link the rings together to make a double chain.

Cut a wire length 1⅜ inches. Thread a ⅛ inch silver bead on the wire between two onyx beads. Loop the ends of the wire.

Join the bead units with the chain.

Disk cutting and punching, p. 40. Filing, p. 12. Sawing, p. 8. Making a wire coil, p. 24. Linking, p. 24.

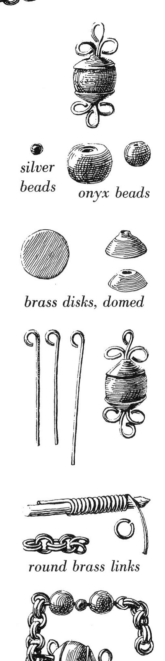

silver beads   onyx beads

brass disks, domed

round brass links

The chain can be any length desired.

Designing

All good designers, consciously or unconsciously, are influenced by the design of the past and by the art forms and practices of their contemporaries.

The designer not only studies the objects made of the material in which he works, but also designs made in other mediums. Natural forms also give him inspiration.

As the fashion in dress changes through the years, so will the styles in jewelry change, but a beautifully designed and well constructed piece of jewelry is always good. It may be laid aside for a time in favor of a newer piece, but will be treasured and worn again, as we might wear our grandmother's charms and lockets with pleasure and pride.

The illustrations on the following pages show a number of designs which may interest the beginner and give him ideas for the use of the materials and the skills which he has learned by following the instructions in this book. They will show him how other designers create original designs, using these same materials and skills.

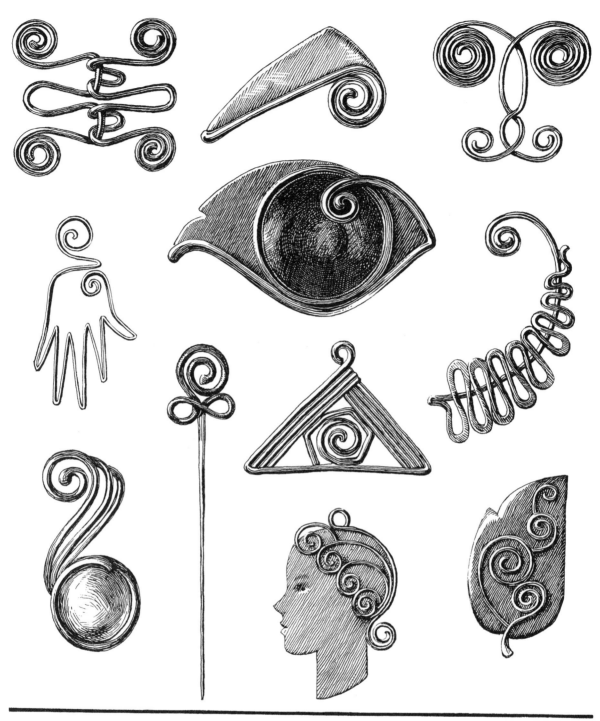

The spiral

The spiral, one of the oldest design motifs, has given pleasure to people for hundreds of years. We find it decorating Grecian pottery, Chinese stone sculpture, primitive wood carving, Spanish iron work and Egyptian and Indian jewelry. We are able to make this form with a wire coil to construct and decorate jewelry.

60

After working in wire, flat and raised metal, beads and disks, and becoming familiar with the possibilities of the material, the shapes and rhythms around us suggest many designs which can be translated into metal and made into jewelry. It is necessary to simplify the real forms. As a rule, the more abstract and symbolic designs are the most interesting.

Things around us

61

Navajo Jewelry

Many of today's craftsmen are inspired by the simple designs of the Navajo jewelry. Over the past hundred years its individuality has remained intact. The Navajo makes handsome jewelry using the more difficult processes of casting and stone setting, but much of their jewelry is of the simple type shown here.

The stamps similar to those used by the Navajos to decorate the surface of their jewelry can be purchased commercially.

As the result of the vision of an American artist and the inherent skill of the Mexican craftsman, the making of silver jewelry has grown to be a fine art and an important industry in Mexico. Many of the designs have been inspired by religious and historic symbols.

The jewelry on this page has been selected for its simple construction from a collection of pieces of great variety and originality.

Mexican
Jewelry

Index

A CATALOG OF SELECTED DOVER
BOOKS IN ALL FIELDS OF INTEREST

CONCERNING THE SPIRITUAL IN ART, Wassily Kandinsky. Pioneering work by father of abstract art. Thoughts on color theory, nature of art. Analysis of earlier masters. 12 illustrations. 80pp. of text. 5⅜ x 8½.   0-486-23411-8

CELTIC ART: The Methods of Construction, George Bain. Simple geometric techniques for making Celtic interlacements, spirals, Kells-type initials, animals, humans, etc. Over 500 illustrations. 160pp. 9 x 12. (Available in U.S. only.)   0-486-22923-8

AN ATLAS OF ANATOMY FOR ARTISTS, Fritz Schider. Most thorough reference work on art anatomy in the world. Hundreds of illustrations, including selections from works by Vesalius, Leonardo, Goya, Ingres, Michelangelo, others. 593 illustrations. 192pp. 7⅛ x 10¼.   0-486-20241-0

CELTIC HAND STROKE-BY-STROKE (Irish Half-Uncial from "The Book of Kells"): An Arthur Baker Calligraphy Manual, Arthur Baker. Complete guide to creating each letter of the alphabet in distinctive Celtic manner. Covers hand position, strokes, pens, inks, paper, more. Illustrated. 48pp. 8¼ x 11.   0-486-24336-2

EASY ORIGAMI, John Montroll. Charming collection of 32 projects (hat, cup, pelican, piano, swan, many more) specially designed for the novice origami hobbyist. Clearly illustrated easy-to-follow instructions insure that even beginning papercrafters will achieve successful results. 48pp. 8¼ x 11.   0-486-27298-2

BLOOMINGDALE'S ILLUSTRATED 1886 CATALOG: Fashions, Dry Goods and Housewares, Bloomingdale Brothers. Famed merchants' extremely rare catalog depicting about 1,700 products: clothing, housewares, firearms, dry goods, jewelry, more. Invaluable for dating, identifying vintage items. Also, copyright-free graphics for artists, designers. Co-published with Henry Ford Museum & Greenfield Village. 160pp. 8¼ x 11.   0-486-25780-0

THE ART OF WORLDLY WISDOM, Baltasar Gracian. "Think with the few and speak with the many," "Friends are a second existence," and "Be able to forget" are among this 1637 volume's 300 pithy maxims. A perfect source of mental and spiritual refreshment, it can be opened at random and appreciated either in brief or at length. 128pp. 5⅜ x 8½.   0-486-44034-6

JOHNSON'S DICTIONARY: A Modern Selection, Samuel Johnson (E. L. McAdam and George Milne, eds.). This modern version reduces the original 1755 edition's 2,300 pages of definitions and literary examples to a more manageable length, retaining the verbal pleasure and historical curiosity of the original. 480pp. 5³⁄₁₆ x 8¼.   0-486-44089-3

ADVENTURES OF HUCKLEBERRY FINN, Mark Twain, Illustrated by E. W. Kemble. A work of eternal richness and complexity, a source of ongoing critical debate, and a literary landmark, Twain's 1885 masterpiece about a barefoot boy's journey of self-discovery has enthralled readers around the world. This handsome clothbound reproduction of the first edition features all 174 of the original black-and-white illustrations. 368pp. 5⅜ x 8½.   0-486-44322-1

LIGHT AND SHADE: A Classic Approach to Three-Dimensional Drawing, Mrs. Mary P. Merrifield. Handy reference clearly demonstrates principles of light and shade by revealing effects of common daylight, sunshine, and candle or artificial light on geometrical solids. 13 plates. 64pp. 5⅜ x 8½. 0-486-44143-1

ASTROLOGY AND ASTRONOMY: A Pictorial Archive of Signs and Symbols, Ernst and Johanna Lehner. Treasure trove of stories, lore, and myth, accompanied by more than 300 rare illustrations of planets, the Milky Way, signs of the zodiac, comets, meteors, and other astronomical phenomena. 192pp. 8⅜ x 11. 0-486-43981-X

JEWELRY MAKING: Techniques for Metal, Tim McCreight. Easy-to-follow instructions and carefully executed illustrations describe tools and techniques, use of gems and enamels, wire inlay, casting, and other topics. 72 line illustrations and diagrams. 176pp. 8¼ x 10⅞. 0-486-44043-5

MAKING BIRDHOUSES: Easy and Advanced Projects, Gladstone Califf. Easy-to-follow instructions include diagrams for everything from a one-room house for bluebirds to a forty-two-room structure for purple martins. 56 plates; 4 figures. 80pp. 8¾ x 6⅜. 0-486-44183-0

LITTLE BOOK OF LOG CABINS: How to Build and Furnish Them, William S. Wicks. Handy how-to manual, with instructions and illustrations for building cabins in the Adirondack style, fireplaces, stairways, furniture, beamed ceilings, and more. 102 line drawings. 96pp. 8¾ x 6⅜. 0-486-44259-4

THE SEASONS OF AMERICA PAST, Eric Sloane. From "sugaring time" and strawberry picking to Indian summer and fall harvest, a whole year's activities described in charming prose and enhanced with 79 of the author's own illustrations. 160pp. 8¼ x 11. 0-486-44220-9

THE METROPOLIS OF TOMORROW, Hugh Ferriss. Generous, prophetic vision of the metropolis of the future, as perceived in 1929. Powerful illustrations of towering structures, wide avenues, and rooftop parks–all features in many of today's modern cities. 59 illustrations. 144pp. 8¼ x 11. 0-486-43727-2

THE PATH TO ROME, Hilaire Belloc. This 1902 memoir abounds in lively vignettes from a vanished time, recounting a pilgrimage on foot across the Alps and Apennines in order to "see all Europe which the Christian Faith has saved." 77 of the author's original line drawings complement his sparkling prose. 272pp. 5⅜ x 8½. 0-486-44001-X

THE HISTORY OF RASSELAS: Prince of Abissinia, Samuel Johnson. Distinguished English writer attacks eighteenth-century optimism and man's unrealistic estimates of what life has to offer. 112pp. 5⅜ x 8½. 0-486-44094-X

A VOYAGE TO ARCTURUS, David Lindsay. A brilliant flight of pure fancy, where wild creatures crowd the fantastic landscape and demented torturers dominate victims with their bizarre mental powers. 272pp. 5⅜ x 8½. 0-486-44198-9

Paperbound unless otherwise indicated. Available at your book dealer, online at **www.doverpublications.com**, or by writing to Dept. GI, Dover Publications, Inc., 31 East 2nd Street, Mineola, NY 11501. For current price information or for free catalogs (please indicate field of interest), write to Dover Publications or log on to **www.doverpublications.com** and see every Dover book in print. Dover publishes more than 500 books each year on science, elementary and advanced mathematics, biology, music, art, literary history, social sciences, and other areas.

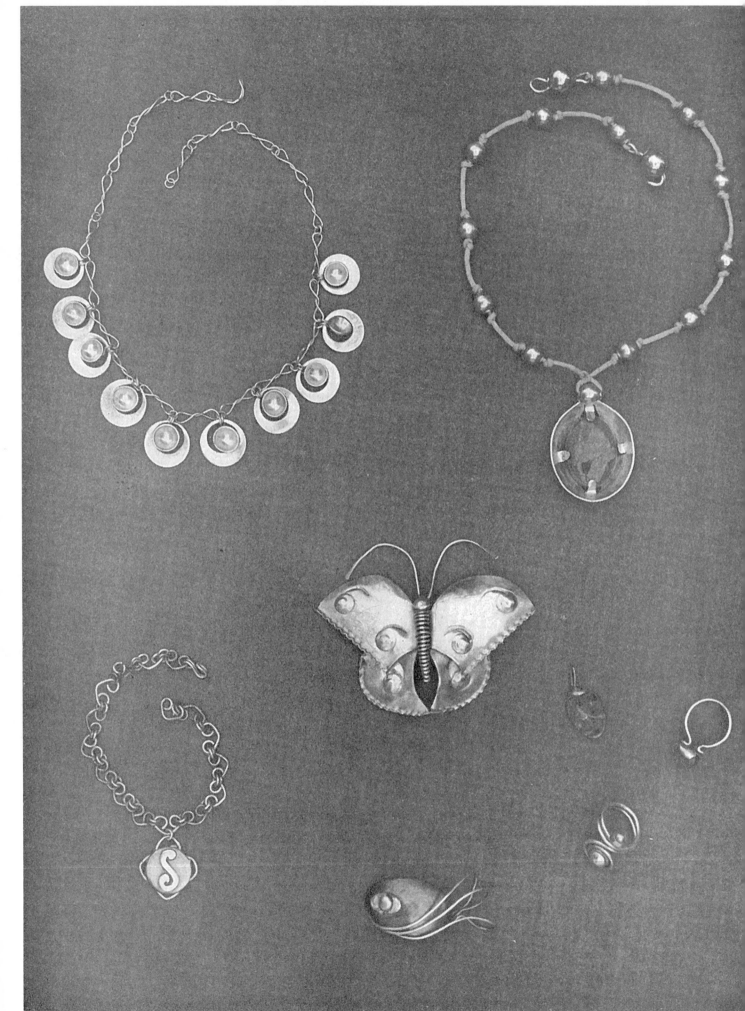